Gothe

During The Pandemic of 2020

Jacqueline Waine

First Edition published in the United Kingdom in 2022 by:

Courtyard Books
Unit 10
The Homend
Shopping Mall
32 The Homend
Ledbury HR8 1BT
www.couryardbooks.co.uk

ISBN: 978-099296036-0

Printed in the United Kingdom by:

In2print Ltd
Phoenix House
Stoke Road
Elmstone Hardwicke
Cheltenham
GL51 9SY
www.in2print.com

Acknowledgements

Many thanks to:-

the many residents and businesses who spent time describing their lockdown memories

the websites and newspapers used while researching this book

Philip Watson for his splendid VE Day photographs

the Old Chapel Committee and the neighbours of the Old Chapel for the renovation photographs

ATW Software Services Ltd, who sponsored this book.

Contents

Part of Gotherington.

Introduction

The last pandemic, over 100 years ago and towards the end of the First World War, to affect this country was known as Spanish Flu. Many men in local villages, towns and cities across the UK, had volunteered or were conscripted to fight for their country and were sent abroad. These exhausted men, and many women, as nurses, returned home at the end of the war, unaware that they might be carriers of diseases. Spanish Flu infected cities, towns and villages across the country. It killed millions worldwide at a time when there was little medical provision. Technology, too, was in its infancy; for instance, the Post Office used telegraphs to send messages and it was not until 1912 that the first telephone exchange was trialled in England.

By the 21st century, the UK had considerably better health care in the form of a free National Health Service (NHS) and local doctors known as General Practitioners (GPs). Unlike one hundred years ago, food is now plentiful and varied and technology has progressed at lightning speed.

However, the pandemic in 2020 came without a quick fix and stretched the Government, its people and NHS almost to breaking point. This is the story of the second pandemic to hit the UK.

2020: The Effect of the Virus Nationally

2020 was a very strange year indeed. It began with rumours of a coming virus. The media informed us that the virus came from a Chinese city called Wuhan. There was speculation that it came from bats or had been created in a laboratory and might be used for chemical warfare. Across this country, many in the population dismissed the news as media hype. It seemed a long way away and unlikely to affect those in the UK. In the past, there had been SARS (Severe Acute Respiratory Syndrome) and MERS (Middle Eastern Respiratory Syndrome) but they had affected people abroad.

However, the Government was aware of the potential seriousness and progress of the virus. It held its first 'COBRA' meeting (**C**abinet **O**ffice **B**riefing **R**ooms, no 'A') on 24th January. These meetings were held to coordinate responses to national and regional emergencies; there was obviously concern. The virus continued to spread and by early March, the World Health Organisation (WHO) declared a worldwide pandemic. This would affect everyone in the UK in one way or another.

Initially, it was publicly known as the 'Corona Virus.' The longer term was Severe Acute Respiratory Syndrome, Corona Virus 2. The shortened term, Corona Virus, caused some mirth as a beer was also known as Corona.

For a while, it was also known by some as 'The Chinese Virus,' but to avoid any association or issue with the Asian community in Britain, the name was eventually changed to Covid-19 (19 after the year 2019 when the virus was first discovered). Likewise, a later variant called the Kent Variant was changed to the Delta Variant so as not to stigmatise people in Kent.

In the early months of 2020, unaware of the dangers, most of the population continued to go to work and behave as normal. The virus could not be seen as it seemed to be carried on the air, but this meant it could easily be transmitted from person to person. Even so, in the early months of the year, there was little panic.

In March, The Cheltenham Races, not far from Gotherington, went ahead as usual. People from all over the UK and Ireland gathered to watch them. It lasted for four days ending on 13th March. It had 15,000 visitors, although not everyone decided to make the journey as approximately 250,000 tickets had been sold. Many of the people in Gotherington either went to the races or played host to the race goers who often came year after year. In Cheltenham, the pubs, restaurants, and shops did a roaring trade, and crowds of people walked up the Evesham Road away from the centre of Cheltenham to the Racecourse.

The Races became one of the hotspots for Covid in Gloucestershire. It was one of the last major sporting events in England to take place before the country was 'locked down'. Sir David King, the government's chief scientific adviser from 2000 to 2007, said it was "the best possible way to accelerate the spread of the virus".[1]

Concern grew and the media began to broadcast the symptoms of Covid to include loss of smell and taste, and breathing difficulties, which could range from mild to deadly. Now everyone was aware of the potential dangers.

The government had already put into action several measures, which included encouraging people to keep two metres apart. To reinforce this, signs went up across the country. Shops immediately limited the numbers of people allowed access at any one time. Surfaces and door handles were regularly disinfected to prevent accidental contamination, although there was no firm evidence that it could be contracted from touching surfaces. The government even suggested people should wash their hands thoroughly in soapy water for the length of time it took to sing 'Happy Birthday' twice.

The Government's initial stance seemed to be to tough it out. They advocated the concept of 'herd immunity', which basically meant the survival rate for people who were vulnerable, such as those who were elderly and/or those with underlying conditions, would be greatly reduced. There was no doubt that these people were disproportionally affected. The recorded numbers of

---

[1] BBC NEWS Hayley Mortimer 30th April 2020

deaths, whether fit or not, began to soar across the country. Each night, the numbers of deaths were broadcast on the News. Experts extrapolated the numbers if the 'herd immunity' policy was continued, and they were huge.

No one knew how far the virus would spread or how severe it would be. There had to be another way to tackle the growing crisis.

Lockdowns, Waves and Tiers

First Lockdown - 2020

On 23rd March in a televised broadcast by the Prime Minister, Boris Johnson announced that there would be a nationwide 'lockdown' effective immediately saying: "From this evening I must give the British people a very simple instruction, you must stay at home." [2] The policy of herd immunity was no more.

Enormous changes began to take place. People were unable to leave their homes except to shop for necessities. They were also not expected to travel to work except if they could not work from home. Exercise at the gym was forbidden and people were only allowed to exercise outside their homes once a day. They could also only travel to a doctor or hospital if medical treatment was required. This was to be enforced by the

---

[2] www.gov.uk/government/speeches

police who were given extra powers to fine people if these exceptions were flouted. To ensure people understood the gravity of the situation, all mobile networks had an alert that said 'Stay at home. Protect the NHS. Save lives.' In April, there was neither a vaccination nor a cure.

Churches

Following the Prime Minister's announcement, the Archbishops and Bishops of the Church of England wrote to their clergy insisting all churches must close. No funerals where to take place inside the churches and baptisms were only to take place in an emergency either in hospital or a person's home.

Doctors and Dentists

Doctors took precautions and rarely saw people face to face. There were appointments held in surgery car parks but not usually inside the surgeries themselves. Instead, diagnoses were made via video links, or if people were concerned, they rang 111 for medical advice. Some people bought their own oxygen level monitors to check the efficiency of their lungs. Others collected them from local GP surgeries and if there was any concern, uploaded their results to their GP's website to be checked.

Understandably, seeing the dentist became impossible so antibiotics were given instead, with teeth usually only being extracted when lockdown eased.

Shops

Large shops and supermarkets introduced one-way systems to ease the flow of people and prevent accidental contact. One text that went round at this time was that a rope and clip on system had been introduced in some shops; it had not. Misinformation was rife. Supermarkets adopted a one in one out approach to stagger the number of people entering the supermarket at any one time. People also took note of how wide the aisles were when considering whether to shop in a particular supermarket and what times would be less busy.

Lorry drivers and shelf packers and other employees were just as susceptible to Covid as everyone else. Supermarkets began to have shortages and some people began to panic buy which left shelves partially empty. Strangely, it was not so much fresh fruit and vegetables, or tinned food and pasta, it was large amounts of toilet paper, despite no evidence that Covid caused bowel or urinary problems. Not so strangely, vast amounts of disinfectant were also snapped up and it was rumoured that some gin makers had turned to making sanitiser. The government appealed to buyers to be more self-controlled as shops were working hard to try and keep up with demand and eventually, reason prevailed.

Many people did not want to queue at the supermarkets in case they caught Covid. Once the UK population became aware that they could order goods online, people did just that. This caused its own problems. Many vulnerable people, isolating in their homes, found they were unable to gain or even to retain delivery slots.

Local independent shops came into their own during this period. People soon realised that they could get their fruit, vegetables, and meat from these rather than face long queues at supermarkets. Small shops often delivered when asked and at times were also able to fulfil orders when the nearby supermarkets could not. The Government insisted nationally that all pubs, clubs, cafes, and restaurants close. Later, lost profits could only be partially recouped by providing takeaway services, which were not prohibited. Locally, this was provided either by The Shutters Inn, or The Smiling Thai. Bookings were taken not face-to-face but via the internet.

By April, people no longer wanted to handle money and supermarkets, takeaways and others were reluctant to accept cash. The answer to this problem was to increase the amount a person could spend on a contactless card from 30 pounds to 45 pounds.

National Health Service
In April, the NHS began contacting those who were vulnerable due to underlying health conditions. It advised these people not to risk mixing with others and asked them to 'shield' for twelve weeks. There were believed to be over a million such people. The NHS also called for people not to contact their doctors if they had not yet received a message to that effect.

The NHS also called for volunteers to help those who were shielding. They were to be called NHS Volunteer Responders. These people could either drive those who were isolating to and from hospital or to and from doctor's appointments or pick up prescriptions or to regularly call them. The NHS wanted a quarter of a million volunteers and set up a link on the internet for people to join. This was in addition to the usual doctors, pharmacies, the NHS 111 telephone line, and other facilities available at the time. It had been recognised that without some support, those who were expected to shield would be unable to do so. This was a national network during the pandemic. It was also to try to keep those who were most vulnerable out of hospital and to stop the NHS becoming overwhelmed.

The Government Health and Social Care Secretary Matt Hancock said:

"In these extraordinary times, it's essential that we all pull together as part of the national effort to protect the most vulnerable, reduce pressures on our NHS and care system and save lives. If you are well and able to do so safely, I would urge you to sign up today to help the most vulnerable people in our communities as an NHS Volunteer Responder."

He continued:

"I am immensely proud of how the whole country is coming together to help one another – we must continue to listen to and live by the latest medical and scientific advice and through this national effort we can truly make a difference."[3]

Despite this, the numbers with Covid infections and those dying still rose.

This had a knock-on effect to NHS workers. They were working long hours and were unable to shop at 'normal' times and often found supermarket shelves were empty by the time they arrived. One nurse appeared on Facebook in tears. She appealed for people to be less selfish as nurses and others were trying to do their work but when they were able to shop there was nothing left for them to buy. This rapidly circulated and was taken up by the media. Supermarkets and others feared the NHS could be overwhelmed not only by the numbers of Covid patients being taken to hospital but also by doctors, nurses and others becoming too exhausted and hungry to continue to work. To tackle this, supermarkets enabled NHS workers to shop at special times. The same principle was also later brought in for the elderly or vulnerable.

On a happier note, each Thursday for ten weeks, those who wanted to take part, stood outside their homes with whistles, saucepans or anything with which they could make a noise, and 'Clapped for Carers,' and the NHS. Often this was the only time people in villages, towns

---

[3] www.nhs.uk/coronavirus or www.gov.uk/coronavirus

and cities across the country were able to go outside other than to exercise and shop for essentials.

Another acknowledgement of the hard work and long hours those working for the NHS were doing was the many rainbow pictures that appeared in windows up and down the country. Bakers quickly realised this and biscuits showing rainbows emerging from clouds began to appear in shops and online.

On 27th March, The Prime Minister was diagnosed with Covid. He was admitted to hospital on 5th April and released on 12th April to recuperate at Chequers. He seemed to have had Covid in a relatively mild form and was luckier than some, saying, in reference to the NHS staff: "I can't thank them enough, I owe them my life."[4] It had now been shown the unseen virus could affect anyone.

In large cities, Nightingale Hospitals were set up to provide extra facilities for those needing critical care. However, the extra hospitals, luckily, were not generally needed. Once in hospital, depending on the level of illness, people could go to intensive care or high dependency units where, to them help breathe, they would be linked to respirators. Sadly, across the country many died.

Queen Elizabeth II, in a rare move, appeared on television. She thanked the continuing work of key

---

[4] Celebrityinsider.org, Suzy Kerr 12th APR 2020

workers, which included those in the NHS and those who were following the social distancing rules.

Work Furlough

Many people were able to work from home, particularly those who could work online, although this did not apply to everyone. If people were 'key' workers, they were expected to continue to go to work, such as doctors and nurses, care workers, some shop workers, those who delivered the post, police, refuse collectors and many others.

For those who were unable to work from home and were not deemed key workers, employers were able to 'furlough' their employees. This was a temporary agreement between employers and employees for the duration of the pandemic. It was either a full-time furlough, or a 'flexible furlough.' If it was a flexible furlough, employees were able to work part of the time but not all the time, as specified in their employment contracts. The arrangement was called the Coronavirus Job Retention Scheme to enable employers to claim a percentage of their employees' normal wages. Chancellor, Rishi Sunak, agreed to pay up to 80 percent or up to a total of £2,500 a month. This meant that people could at least still be paid something. Even so, many people across the country were unable to retain their jobs and became unemployed. Later, to avoid an economic crisis, the self-employed were also included in the scheme.

Education

Schools were told to close, but staff had to continue teaching in one form or another. For all schools, normal face-to-face teaching was deemed impossible. The only way to deliver lessons was remotely, either providing teaching online or, if a family did not possess a laptop, as nationally it was found many did not, staff dropped off material or provided a school laptop on a temporary basis.

However, the children of key workers, whether at nursery, primary or secondary schools, to keep the country running, were to continue to attend their schools albeit, because of reduced numbers, part-time, in mixed ages and/or ability classes.

For the older children, the GCSEs or A Levels that they should have taken in 2020 were put on hold. The Education Minister, Gavin Williamson, decided to use an algorithm to predict the GCSE results as children had not been able to attend school in the normal way. This decision was criticised by the teaching profession, teaching unions and some families. Teachers believed their continued professional assessment of children's grades were not considered and the children's work was thus downgraded. Eventually, the algorithmic process was withdrawn as it was found that nationally, some grades were indeed not based on the child's ability but on other factors. Instead of the algorithm, teachers were allowed to give grades based on the children's work and their anticipated grades.

Lockdown also affected young adults at university. Universities and colleges continued to teach but they taught exclusively online.

Garages

Many garages took advice from the Independent Garage Association (IGA), who in turn, took their advice from the government. The government was considering extending the yearly MOT (Ministry of Transport) test, an audit of vehicles road worthiness. The idea was to extend the period by six months to cater for the lockdown period. However, the IGA was not in agreement with the government and wanted the extension to be shorter. The IGA was concerned that by extending MOTs by six months, generally carried out by their members, and equating to 80 percent or the equivalent of 30 million vehicles each year in the UK, this would have a serious impact on the cash flow of garages. The result of an extension would be to create peaks and troughs in income. Despite these concerns, the MOT extension went ahead and was extended by six months.[5]

Face masks also became mandatory for garage employees when interacting with their customers. If this was not followed, the fine was up to £10,000. However, fewer people travelled far which meant fewer cars on the road and thus fewer accidents or break downs and the consequent need to visit garages.

---

[5] IGA, 26th March 2020

Kennels/ Kennel Club

Kennels and catteries much like other businesses or clubs often join associations to give them advice. The Kennel Club was one such, for breeders of pedigree dogs.

At the beginning of 2020, the main event for the Kennel Club was Crufts. It began in 1891 and had only been interrupted for the duration of the two World Wars. The Kennel Club attracts vast numbers of dog lovers and those selling merchandise. Each year, the owners of pedigree dogs exhibit their dogs in breed categories and compete for an overall 'Best in Show'. As well as this, there is a category for dogs that help people.

In 2020, the show was due to be held at the NEC in Birmingham and was expected to run from 5th to 8th March. Public Health England had advised the Kennel Club not to cancel the event. The main message was to ensure personal hygiene by following the government's advice, 'Catch it. Bin it. Kill it.' At the same time the organisers also expected everyone to follow any travel restrictions and isolation, advice laid out by the government and that given by the World Health Organisation.[6]

---

[6] www.gov.uk/guidance/coronavirus-covid-19-information-for-the-public and www.who.int/emergencies/diseases/novel-coronavirus-2019/advice-for-public

As the virus progressed, concern grew that pets, as well as people, might catch it and pass it on to their owners. This would have had a knock-on effect to all pet owners and people who owned kennels and catteries which might have resulted in wide scale culling. However, this possibility was robustly denied by The World Health Organisation, which stated:

"At present, there is no evidence that companion animals/pets such as dogs or cats can be infected with the new Corona virus."

This must have come as a great relief to many.

The Kennel Club continued to liaise with the Department for Environment, Food, and Rural Affairs (Defra), and by 13th May, it announced that due to the continuing pandemic, all clubs, societies and events should be cancelled until the end of September. Nationwide kennels either closed or reduced their services and could no-longer 'show' their dogs.

Clubs

All clubs, whatever they were, nationally or locally, whether held in spacious Village Halls or not, also had to close.

By Easter, the Queen went on the television to try to raise the nation's morale. Her Easter message, stated: "Corona virus will not overcome us." However, by the end of April, a minute's silence was held across the country, for all the key workers who had caught the virus and died.

By May, the death toll in the UK outstripped Europe. Across the country, the Office of National Statistics showed that a third of the deaths were in care homes for the elderly.[7]

Victory in Europe Day (VE Day)

May 2020 brought the 75th anniversary of Victory in Europe Day (VE Day). Held annually, it was to commemorate those who had fought in Europe in the Second World War. It had first taken place on May 8th 1945, when Germany surrendered to the Allies, (these included the United Kingdom, much of Europe, Russia and America). However, the war continued until 15th August in the Far East when the Emperor of Japan surrendered. This is known as 'Victory in Japan Day' (VJ Day, also called Victory in the Pacific) and is commemorated to acknowledge those who had fought in the Pacific region.

In 2020, the country was supposed to celebrate VE Day. It was a special anniversary and larger celebrations than usual were planned in the capital. The Queen was to lead the country's celebrations and give a speech on the television and there were also to be street parties and parades across the country with an extra Bank Holiday. However, due to the pandemic, the large-scale celebrations were cancelled.

---

[7]www.ons.gov.uk

Instead, the Culture Secretary, Oliver Dowden, on behalf of the Government, announced that any celebrations were to take place 'on our doorsteps.'[8] These celebrations therefore had to be low key and socially distanced.

Despite the sunny weather, things seemed to be getting worse with numbers of infections and deaths rising. On May 10th, the Government changed its slogan for England from, "Stay Home. Protect the NHS. Save Lives," to "Stay Alert. Control the Virus. Saves Lives." The government also extended the furlough system to October, much to the relief of many people.

Staying at home was not faithfully followed by everyone. In May and beyond, the media was full of the trip taken by the Prime Minister's special political

---

[8] Evening Standard, Kit Heren 7th May 2020

advisor, Dominic Cummings. He was alleged to have driven from London to Barnard Castle in Durham, approximately 255 miles for childcare, despite the Government edict to stay at home and not to take unnecessary trips.

Later in the month, the NHS introduced a Contact Tracing System. This was an attempt to stop Covid spreading. It was to trace those who have been infected and trace those who had been in their vicinity, they were then expected to self-isolate. Strangely, even those living in the same household did not necessarily catch Covid.

Relaxation - 2020

At the end of May, the Prime Minister announced that the previous restrictions could be relaxed. Dominic Raab, Secretary of State for Foreign Commonwealth and Development Affairs, told Sophy Ridge of Sky News, "the country could not stay in lockdown forever."[9] There was still no cure or vaccine and not all medical advisors agreed with his general outlook.

This relaxation meant that those whom the NHS had flagged as clinically extremely vulnerable, were able, after 10 weeks inside their homes and gardens, to go outside if they so wished. Yet, many older and/or vulnerable residents and even some who were neither, preferred to stay at home. They were extremely

---

9 Sky News Sophy Ridge 1 June 2020. Medical News Today Hannah Flynn 28th October 2021

concerned about meeting anyone or shopping, preferring instead to continue to isolate.

Education then became a priority for the Government as schools had been closed since 23rd March and continued online. The Secretary of State for Education stated that from the beginning of June, primary schools should reopen before the summer break. This was to enable schools to take 'bubbles' (groups) of Reception children and those in Years One and Six. However, the Governmental proposal was rejected by many head teachers and teaching unions as they felt this did not take account of social distancing. To accommodate an average class size of 30 children, the classroom space would have to double, or the class size reduced to 15 to avoid transmission. This was not possible for most schools. Nor did it take account of the availability of teachers, who were just as likely as anyone else to contract Covid. After due consideration, the decision was reversed.

By mid-June, the government felt that Covid was no longer the threat it had been. Now, people were able to travel further than the immediate neighbourhood. However, without the footfall of customers, many shops were empty or had closed. People, at last, were able to buy things from actual rather than virtual shops, although shops only allowed a limited number of people inside at any one time which could result in long queues standing outside.

That month, the 'two metre' rule was relaxed in England to become the 'one metre plus rule.' In towns and cities across the country, signs were painted on pavements to create one-way systems and bollards put up on the edges of roads to protect people from passing traffic as they politely stepped aside to avoid others.

People who had previously been restricted to one household were now allowed to visit each other and to stay overnight. Many whose careers had taken them to large towns and cities, had not been able to visit their families or friends for many months. The relaxation of the rules brought an influx of friends and relatives eager to see their loved ones. June 23rd was the hottest day of the year so far.

The Government, throughout the summer, promoted a scheme to help hospitality, which had been badly hit by the pandemic. This was called, 'Eat out to help out.' The Chancellor of the Exchequer was filmed waiting at tables in London, to help to get the message across. The government, under this scheme, provided 50 percent of the cost for non-alcoholic drinks and food at the participating venues. The only stipulation was that meals and drinks had to be eaten on the premises.

Those that caught Covid, now had to isolate for 10 days after testing positive. In July, the Prime Minister suggested there would be a 'significant return to normality' by Christmas. Employers were given more discretion regarding workers' pay, which could mean statutory sick pay instead of normal wages. Restrictions continued to ease, with more venues opening. There was still no vaccine.

The virus was airborne so the government decided that from 24th July 2020 onwards, face masks should be made compulsory in supermarkets and shops. This created a thriving trade in making and selling masks.
Supermarkets now had masks for sale at their entrances if anyone had forgotten to bring one.

Buses continued to run but were often largely empty despite residents now being able to take non-essential journeys. The weather continued to be glorious, but in the ongoing dry hot weather, wheat production was becoming a problem and consequently the supply of flour was well down.

By mid-August, older children obtained their 'A' Level and GCSE results based on teacher predictions rather than examinations, which made some very happy while others less so. By late September, university students began returning to their universities as well, but the numbers of Covid infections continued to rise.

The Second Wave - 2020
By September, a second wave of the virus was upon the country. The virus had now mutated into what was initially called 'the Kent' variant, as it was found in Kent. As previously the case, this name was quickly changed after an outcry from those in Kent. Thus, it became known as the Delta Variant.

Towards the end of the month, Michael Gove, representing the Government, recommended that, if possible, people should again work from home. To support this, the following month the Chancellor announced that if employers had to close their businesses due to the pandemic, then the government would pay two thirds of what those employed should receive. The Government, on the advice of SAGE, also implemented 'the rule of six.' This meant that no more than six people could meet, with a few exceptions such as team games.

Things seemed to go from bad to worse. The weather in early October was appalling and 3rd October was recorded as the wettest day on record that year. Covid cases were also rising rapidly, so by the end of the month, the Prime Minister agreed to a four-week lockdown. This would be from the 5th of November through to the first week of December. For those in employment, the government also extended the furlough scheme until March 2021.

Tiers - 2020

On 17th October 2020, a new system was introduced, comprising of Three Tiers, Gloucestershire was placed in Tier Two. This was a high alert and meant that only up to six people could meet outside but they had to remain socially distanced. To meet inside meant only those in the usual household or support bubble. Travelling was only allowable if it enabled people to continue working or if it was not possible for a person to work from home, with another exception being shopping.

At this point, restaurants could only offer a takeaway service. Pubs were open but they could only provide alcoholic drinks with a 'substantial meal.' Quite what the definition of this was, was met with much hilarity as Michael Gove, responsible for the Cabinet Office, National Security and Civil Contingencies and tackling Covid-19, suggested a substantial meal could be a single Scotch egg.

There was also some confusion about exercising. Indoor sports could only take place if there was no interaction. This was the same for places of worship if they decided to open. For weddings or civil partnership ceremonies, only 15 people could attend which rose to a maximum of 30 for a funeral, with only 15 for a wake which could not be held in a person's home.

Now people were able to visit care homes if the resident was at the end of their life and provided the visitor tested negative for Covid. Those, who the NHS considered clinically extremely vulnerable or had been advised to shield, could meet five others outside, although they were advised against it.

Second Lockdown - 2020
The Prime Minister announced a second national lockdown for England in October 2020. Now pubs, restaurants, gyms, and non-essential shops had to close

again, this time for four weeks although schools, colleges and universities did not have to.

Meanwhile, in November, unbeknownst to the population, vaccine trials, developed by Pfizer/BioNTECH, had been successful. There seemed to be some light at the end of the tunnel. At the beginning of December, the BBC announced that the research had been fast tracked and had only taken 10 months from the idea to creating a vaccine. This made some people wary, suggesting that it was unlikely to be safe, but the reality was that the vaccine had been an extension of many years of research and development into vaccines.

The Prime Minister hoped that after 2nd December, the restrictions put in place would be eased and regions would go back to the tiered system, saying:

"Christmas is going to be different this year, perhaps very different, but it's my sincere hope and belief that by taking tough action now, we can allow families across the country to be together."

From 5th November to 2nd December, Gloucestershire remained in Tier Two. The situation was reviewed on 16th December. The expectation was that families would be able to spend Christmas together. However, Christmas celebrations were now in jeopardy as new infections began to rise. The government announced that only three households could get together a create a 'Christmas Bubble' from the 23rd to the 27th December

2020. This created difficulties for large extended families and those who lived far away and meant many would be unable to meet. Another restriction was that those who intended to visit from London were not able to during the Christmas period as the Covid rate there was so high.

On Boxing Day, 26th December, Matt Hancock announced that those areas previously deemed to be in Tier Two would now be in Tier Three; this included Gloucestershire, London was now in the newly created Tier Four.

Tier Three represented a very high alert. This meant more care had to be taken and that people could not be invited indoors. Hospitality could now only offer a takeaway service again and weddings were unable to offer a reception and wakes could not be indoors. Those who were considered clinically extremely vulnerable or had been advised to shield were no longer expected to venture outside and, instead, were expected to shop online or if help was not available, to ring the NHS volunteers help line. For some people, this meant they had to either cut short their Christmas celebrations and leave or decide to stay before lockdown came into force.

Numbers of infections continued to rise. The Office for National Statistics suggested over a million people in England had Covid between the 27th December and 2nd January. By the 28th of December, the number of people in hospitals infected with Covid-19 was above that experienced in April and numbers of new infections continued to rise.[10]

On the 30th of December, a second vaccine, developed by Oxford AstraZeneca, was approved. The Health Minister gave the go ahead for the NHS to provide vaccinations. The date that the first vaccine was to be given was chosen to be the 4th of January 2021 and this was to be televised.

On this day, Margaret Keenan became the first person in the world to receive the Pfizer/BioNTECH vaccine. Great hope was attached to this event.

A third lockdown came into operation on the 6th of January 2021.

---

[10] www.ons.gov.uk

Gotherington Memories

Memories Introduction

This is a collection of memories in the lockdown year of 2020 from the village of Gotherington in northern Gloucestershire.

The village is bordered by arable fields or pastures for grazing animals. It is normally tranquil and quiet. In the daytime, many of the residents commute to work and families take their children to the village school. This means the village is largely silent during the day accompanied by the distant hum of traffic from the

Evesham Road (A435) and the motorway (M5) beyond it, both to the west.

There are no streetlights, meaning the darkness in the village benefits the nocturnal creatures and it is possible to see a carpet of stars on a clear night. However, in the distance, the towns of Cheltenham and Tewkesbury, and nearby, the large village of Bishops Cleeve, all cast their glow in the sky.

In Gotherington, there is a village shop and post office, The Shutters Inn, a plant nursery, and a nursery school together with a primary school. There is also a village hall and Freeman's Field, otherwise known as the playing fields, with its tennis pavilion and courts, and the Rex Rhodes building. Further along the village, there is also a converted chapel (known as the Old Chapel) which is secular and holds some village events and clubs. There is no church in the village.

The road running through Gotherington is called Malleson Road on one side of the Old Chapel and on the other it, becomes Gretton Road and leads to Winchcombe in the east. Another smaller road, Gotherington Lane, links Gotherington to Woodmancote and Bishops Cleeve towards the south. Here are pubs, supermarkets, a grocer, butchers, chemists, doctors, dentists, an optician, village halls, a large church (St Michael and All Angels), primary schools and a secondary school together with lots of houses, all just over a mile away.

To the north is the village of Woolstone. This runs along the side of Crane Hill and Woolstone Hill. It is a smaller village than Gotherington and is linked by Woolstone Lane. This meanders from Gotherington to Woolstone, a mere three quarters of a mile away. The village has no amenities other than the church, St. Martin de Tour.

Another means of travel is across the fields following the footpaths from Gotherington to Bishops Cleeve, one of which is known by some as the 'coffin path.' From Gotherington to Woolstone cross the fields there are also little wooden bridges over the Tirle Brook.

By March 2020. these villages, although not far from Cheltenham and Tewkesbury, were effectively cut off from the towns and cities beyond. The only contact with the outside world was by telephone or via electronic means or a quick trip to the shops.

Here in Gotherington, during the lockdown, the community pulled together. There was a sense of purpose. People checked on their neighbours and anyone they felt to be isolated, elderly, and/or vulnerable.

People were more than happy to provide help and support 'at a distance' or online, such as shopping, if it was wanted. This ranged from food deliveries to spiritual support, either online or by telephone, provided by the Vicar, The Reverend, Richard Reakes. Of course, this did not stop many, particularly those living on their own, still feeling lonely and isolated. No-one knew how long the situation would last, a couple of weeks or months or may be even years.

In Gotherington, if people became seriously ill, they would go to Cheltenham, Gloucester Royal Hospital or Tewkesbury Hospitals. Some long-term residents did become ill and sadly died. An example of this was in The Lawns where people came onto the street to show a collective, socially distanced, mark of respect. The hearse drove to the front of the person's house, stopped then slowly moved off to the Crematorium in Cheltenham.

Gotherington Organisations and Businesses

This next section looks specifically at some of the organisations and businesses in Gotherington.

Gotherington Parish Council

The Parish Council normally held meetings in the Village Hall once a month with at times one or two Borough Councillors. During the pandemic, initially the meetings continued in person, with the exceptions, due to training, of February and April. As time rolled on and the situation worsened, the Parish and Borough Councils, in Tewkesbury, began working online and from home. Members of the public could no longer attend meetings in person, although often no members of the public had been present at all, now the public could only attend virtually.

During 2020, the numbers of Parish Councillors wavered too and were often as low as four. One Parish Councillor, who had not attended or sent any apologies for six consecutive months, was removed from the Council. The Clerk had also gone, and it took several months before suitable replacements could be appointed.

Most months there were regular issues; proposals for local housing developments, potholes, footpath repairs, grass cutting, fencing disputes, the growth of ivy on trees, together with what should be done to the memorial and who was responsible for its upkeep. Further afield, discussions also revolved round the expected large-scale housing and cyber park developments in Cheltenham and the inevitable impact on local schools further afield, such as Gotherington.

In March 2020, a relatively local event took place; Cheltenham Races, just beyond Gotherington. This is held annually and attracts large crowds. The races were a particular problem for the Parish Council as cars often sped through the village.

That year one notable proposal by the Parish Council was a special litter pick in memory of Ian Wilson. He had been a stalwart litter picker throughout the village and along the roads around Gotherington for many years. Unfortunately, later minutes did not mention this proposal again and with other more pressing events nationally, this idea was dropped.

By June 2020, the Parish Council were getting daily updates about Covid, both in Gloucestershire and nationally. The hope was still to hold some events on Freeman's Field, but these would have to be subject to Covid related restrictions so distancing signs were acquired by the Chairman of the Parish Council and dotted about the village.

There were also Zoom meetings about further proposed
and opposed housing developments on the
Meadow/Cooks Field. One woman spoke on behalf of
the residents and Simon Tarling spoke on behalf of the
Parish Council, both of whom opposed the development.
There were also safety concerns about building 15
houses on Malleson Road, so the Highways Safety
Scheme had to be consulted and these and other

negotiations with various developers continued throughout the year.

Gotherington, Oxenton, Woolstone Neighbourhood Scheme (GOWNS).

Throughout this turbulent time, GOWNS were busy, not only delivering goods themselves but also supplying everyone in the village with a list of contacts for various shops and services. These were both those in the village as well as those in the surrounding villages and as far away as Cheltenham. Butchers, and grocers, cheese from the local Cheeseman and plants from Gotherington Plant Nursery, pharmacies in Bishops Cleeve, even Gotherington Cross Garage offered their services. They all offered online, or telephone contacts and one person even offered her IT skills to anyone having trouble with their equipment or who wanted someone to set it up for them.

Churches

Reverend Richard Reakes was the Team Vicar of Bishops Cleeve (St Michael and All Angels), Woolstone (St Martin de Tour), Oxenton (St John the Baptist) and Southam (Church of Ascention), as well as Gotherington. He could no longer conduct face to face meetings or services for the members of his congregation. Instead, this all went online or by telephone.

Woolstone (St Martin de Tour) the nearest church.

Gotherington Primary School (Academy)

Like all schools, they had a directive in March from Government via the local education authority (LEA) to close. This gave the head teacher and staff two days' notice. At this time, everything was constantly changing with updates from the LEA. The head teacher then had to write a remote teaching and learning policy. This meant the teaching staff had to create home learning packs and provide videos so their classes could continue to learn. The school wanted families to keep in touch and to give as much feedback as possible so they could change things if necessary.

The school was then only open for key workers' children and those that were deemed vulnerable in some way. However, because so many parents were key workers, the intake grew and grew until it was nearly 50 percent of normal attendance. Parents and the school soon realised how difficult it would be to keep everyone happy, so parents became very good at only sending their children to school if they had to work, either remotely from home or go in to work, even if it was only part time. The head teacher felt the staff were incredibly lucky that they were so supported by the children's parents. The school is also in a cluster group of schools, so were able to Zoom each other which was very supportive.

Initially, only Reception and Year Six were allowed back to school, and only a maximum 15 in a group. All doors were opened to enable the air to circulate, and sinks were installed outdoors to be used at playtimes. As the school is an academy, they did not first have to get permission from the LEA so could act somewhat independently.

That year, no SATs took place although they did keep the phonics screening. Year Six sadly were not able to have a residential trip or have an actual Leavers Assembly as this had to be online.

The head teacher felt the school did its best in the circumstances as a team and as a community, they were she said; "really lucky."

Outside the school a 'snake/caterpillar,' of brightly painted pebbles grew along the pavement, left by parents and children as they walked past.

Garden House Nursery School

The small nursery school is at the back of the village hall, in the Rex Rhodes building. It has a patch of fenced in ground for the children to be supervised outside.

The nursery is run independently from Gotherington Primary School by two women and their staff of seven who have worked together for many years. They look after children from two years old to Reception age. The nursery itself runs on Montessori principles and as such there is no computer or television. Instead, they believe this approach enables the children to develop their own thinking, language, social and dexterity skills and encourages a growing independence in readiness for school.

They also have an After School Club of older children who, before lockdown, could be seen walking in a long crocodile, down the road from Gotherington Primary School to the nursery school accompanied by the nursery school staff, where they could await their parents. This is registered for 24 under eights and some older children. All this stopped with the announcement of lockdown.

Clubs

Once the Government had made their announcement in March, the Village Sports Subcommittee decided that the various activities that usually took place on Freeman's Field, should stop. The upgrade pencilled in for the tennis courts was put back to 2021 and any club's fees, such as for the footballers and cricket club were reduced.

At the same time, any clubs that took place in the village hall were also cancelled, although some continued online, such as the Brownies.

Gotherington Stores

The shop, had been suffering from falling sales before lockdown and was only open from 9 a.m. to 4.30 p.m. It had changed from a general shop with a Post Office to a café with Post Office

Once lockdown took place, there were no customers at all. The village shop owner found that once schools closed and the Government announced people had to work from home, if they could, there was no longer any passing trade. The AirBnB above the shop also lost its income so, unfortunately, the shop closed.

The Shutters Inn

At the pub, the weeks leading up to lockdown had been busy. With Cheltenham Race Week, particularly at breakfast time, it looked as though it was going to be their busiest year to date. Then came lockdown.

There were no deliveries and 38 barrels of beer had to be destroyed. They had to be poured down the drain. Permission for the disposal had to be sought from Severn Trent. Photographs also had to be taken to ensure it was done properly, which it was. Then the cellar was powered down. There was also the question of the fruit and vegetables bought to cater for the influx of expected race goers. Any stock that could not be used was given to the community via GOWNS. GOWNS then gave the fresh fruit and vegetables to those who were isolating or vulnerable.

The couple, like everyone else who had children, had to home school their three different aged children. They found this hard and felt their year six child missed out on his end of primary school experience.

The couple decorated the windows for VE Day but they did not go out. They also clapped for the NHS and saw their neighbours coming out to do it as well, which they felt was nice.

Central Cross Garage

For this family run business, it was a very stressful time. Most of the mechanics had to be furloughed once lockdown was announced. It was lucky that the business was family run as otherwise it would have gone under despite the government grant. Up until then, they were doing MOTs and repairs, then the government deferred MOTs for six months. The only work available was the repair of cars for key workers, such as doctors and nurses. No-one else was driving anywhere so very few people needed the garage.

The family were often stopped by the police when they were on their way to work. The police were near Bishops Cleeve and Toddington roundabout on the Evesham Road checking people were not taking unnecessary journeys and could issue fines for unnecessary trips. Eventually, the family, who all went to work in one car, had to have a pass and made one for the mechanics so that they were able to come to work without the constant worry of being stopped and fined.

Gotherington Plant Nursery

The government initially banned all 'non-essential' retail in the UK to stop the spread of Covid. This announcement included plant nurseries as well as other retail outlets. James Barnes the chair of The

Horticultural Trades Association (HTA) said on the Today Programme,

"Growers will have spent the last three or four months building up supplies which they can't sell. If they can't sell it, it can't get to the end user, it can't get in the ground, then it has to be written off. They'll (the plants) have to be literally thrown away."[11]

The HTA, in conjunction with the government, considered how to prevent this and provide financial support for the nations plant nurseries.

In the meantime, many nurseries including Gotherington Plant Nursery investigated 'Click and Collect,' a method whereby customers can order online and pick up their items later or have them delivered. This went from strength to strength.

Springfield Kennels & Cattery
Like all kennels, Springfield Kennels was affected during 2020. They were only able to groom dogs for health reasons. The kennels were closed but bills still

---

[11] 31 March 2020 The Today Programme

had to be paid, luckily their staff could be furloughed.

Old Chapel

The Old Chapel had been bought in November 2018 and
was due to be renovated in 2020. Initially, in 2018 it
was offered to the Parish Council, but they turned it
down, and, as a result, a consortium of local people
bought it. They, in turn, set it up as a charity and
became its trustees who went on to raise money for its
renovation.

Various clubs were held on the premises, but at the
beginning of March 2020, all the clubs and events held
in the Old Chapel, like everywhere else, stopped and its
doors were closed and locked. Then, only the occasional
visitor entered it, for instance, to decorate the front

windows which sported a large rainbow in support of the NHS.

Once lockdown was relaxed, the weather was so good the trustees of the Old Chapel took advantage of this and outside renovations of the building began in earnest. Snape, the builders, put up scaffolding and removed the cladding on the outside walls. This allowed them to breathe and the builders to look at the brickwork underneath the render. Some of the brickwork had crumbled so it was repointed then a new breathable cladding applied on top.

The roof, too, had to be removed. It had previously been covered with heavy tiles which, over the years, made the walls begin to bow outward. A crane removed the tiles and the old wooden joists, and new joists and lighter slate tiles put in place. Many of these tiles were sponsored and the sponsors names added to the tile and a record kept. The tiles raised £4000, which was the equivalent to half a roof.

The Old Chapel also provided teas and coffees after the annual Service of Remembrance. This was held around the memorial in the middle of the village, to commemorate those who had given their lives in the First and Second World Wars and those who had fought and died in conflicts around the world since.

In November 2020, no Remembrance Service was held. The vicar would normally stand at the entrance of the Old Chapel, opposite the War Memorial, to give his service and a crowd would form and various local representatives of the armed forces and other organisations would lay wreaths.

After the service, teas and coffees would be served inside the Old Chapel. In 2020, the Old Chapel was shut. However, so that the fallen were not forgotten, a string of knitted poppies were wound along the railings. Knitted poppies to commemorate the fallen in both world wars appeared at Woolstone and Oxenton churches as well.

Villagers' Memories

The next section recounts the memories of those in Gotherington who agreed to be interviewed. In general, the memories are anonymous although some people are identifiable by their occupations or posts.

These memories are across the age range and includes those living alone to those living as couples or in families as well as those with a variety of occupations and those with none. There are often common themes.

In the village, we obeyed the rules set down by the Government as best we could and hunkered down. These are people's memories:

Memory 1

The couple in the shop found home schooling their children and running a shop and post office very difficult. They could no longer rely on their older relatives, who used to collect their children from a school outside the village. It was now no longer an option as no-one was supposed to travel and many older people were isolating.

As things eased, she said that fewer and fewer people came into the shop and when they did, people did not always obey the new rules of keeping their distance and wearing masks. Eventually, the shop was stripped of everything except the Post Office and the banking service which had become very important to the older residents. Despite this, the revenue kept going down. Eventually they had to make a decision which was hard for them. Despite the shop being an essential service to the village, they felt they had no real choice and the shop closed.

Memory 2

One mother felt that the timing of the school lockdown, at the beginning of March, worked well for her family. Although she felt the decision to shut schools was very quick, but it also meant that there was no time to dread it.

One to one attention worked well with her two boys. It worked particularly well for the younger boy. They were both keen and did any homework that the school provided. However, lockdown also made the family decide to change school for their older child. Lockdown gave them the time to consider what would be best in the long run. It had been difficult to get him into school in the mornings so a change would give him a new start. Once schools opened again, he was able to start at the new school at the beginning of the new academic year.

Her husband usually drove 40 to 50,000 miles a year for work but all that stopped. During lockdown, he did not have to travel at all. It made them take stock. She had been worried about him burning out and did not want him to work so hard. They considered all the ins and outs of their lifestyle and decided they could ride it out if he worked shorter hours from home, so they bought office furniture and set up a work area. He worked from home and the boys got used to seeing him working and being there. He would stop at five o'clock and as the weather was so good, they would have a family barbeque. They spent much of their time outside in the garden and had most of their meals on their patio; it almost doubled their living space.

The family loved not having the old routine. Everything was cancelled, even the swimming lessons they had organised, so the boys learnt to swim in their own swimming pool. Come six o'clock, her husband stopped working and they had gin and tonics over the fence with their neighbour, it became quite a regular thing. The neighbours started making sour dough bread and the starter was christened 'Steve the Sour Dough Starter'.

'We loved the sensation of not going anywhere. It was so nice not to clock watch and not to have to put on makeup,' she said. She also appreciated how quiet it was. The boys were allowed to ride their bikes around The Lawns too as there were no cars about. It reminded her of when she was young.

She also joined GOWNS because she wanted to do something to help. Everyone was registered and DBS checked, and everyone seemed grateful for their deliveries. She delivered to one man who had ordered steak, dressed crab and wine. She also regularly telephoned her neighbour and did her shopping, and they became friends. She thought it gave her neighbour a lot of comfort knowing they were there.

Her grandmother had previously put herself in a care home. She was very outgoing and loved nice things. To start with, she had lots of visitors but all that stopped with lockdown. After that, she went downhill rapidly. Her death certificate said 'Covid', but the family was not sure it was just that. The funeral was not what her grandmother would have wanted. Not many people were allowed to attend the funeral. Instead, it was watched by some on Zoom. It was a shame because online, people are not aware of the others watching. It was a low point for all the family, but they rang round and got dressed up and raised a glass of pink champagne in her memory which she would have loved.

On a happier note, on VE Day, the family sat outside and chatted with their neighbours. They also did the NHS clap and waved at each other. It seemed louder in the lower part of the village, but we felt we were all in this together.

They had thought they might move, but lockdown made them appreciate what they had, for instance, all the walks and lovely neighbours. She said 'it was lovely to sit and chat with all the people that we knew. Although we would not want to go back, it was a lovely experience. It was all positive for us. We are very grateful for where we live.'

She felt that everyone was in the same storm but in different boats and that would have affected how they viewed lockdown.

Memory 3

The Races are an annual event held on the edge of Cheltenham. This was this woman's second year at the Races with nine friends. Her husband had heard rumours about a virus, but they only seemed to be vague and far away. The government had remained quiet, so she assumed there was nothing to worry about.

Ten of them had breakfast in Cheltenham. The cafes were crowded and so were the streets. They, along with hordes of other people, took the long walk from the town centre up to the racecourse. The crowds were jolly, everyone seemed happy.

She only went for one day. The previous year, she and her friends had spent a lot of time in the very crowded Champagne Bar. In 2020, they stayed outside on the stands. Some people were coughing but she was not concerned and thought it was only to be expected at that time of year.

The next day, she had a sore throat and her friends developed 'colds or 'flu'. Her husband, who had not gone to the Races, was laid low for a week, with what they thought was 'flu. One of their number, who was usually the life and soul of the party had been particularly subdued at the Races. She was taken to hospital the day after and was diagnosed with Covid-19.

Sadly, she was one of the first in the county to die from the virus. Whether or not her friends had Covid-19 before the races, and whether the friends and her husband had caught the virus there, she will never know.

By the middle of spring, the weather was glorious. It was dry and sunny and seemed to go on for weeks. She and her husband spent most of their time in the garden. She said, 'it will never look so good again!'

Her husband was unable to work and so furloughed all his staff. They could not go anywhere, but as there were two of them, they kept each other company. They bought their shopping online, as she was classed as 'clinically vulnerable'. She researched one side of her family history using Ancestry and completed a dissertation for an MA History online through Birmingham University.

Their two adult children, like many others in the village, lived in London and could not visit. Both lived in small flats, which made having a garden and living in the countryside a real bonus for the couple. They missed their children and worried about them, particularly their daughter who worked for a London hospital. It was not until the summer, when lockdown was relaxed for the first time, that their children were able to visit. Their son, who worked online, visited, and stayed for a year!

Memory 4

Before the lockdown, one woman talked of having a full week of meetings ahead of her. Once lockdown was announced, all the face-to-face meetings were cancelled, and she had to go online instead.

She researched into the houses in the village and the ancestry of the older established families who had lived in Gotherington for generations. Her research included photographs and can now be accessed through the Gotherington village website. She also created a World War Two trail saying: 'It was something to focus on and once people are able to get out and about again, they can follow the trail if they want to.'

She also supported her elderly parents who lived in the village. There were times when they needed to see a doctor in nearby Bishops Cleeve, which she said of the surgery, 'I couldn't have wished for better.' She was very happy with the service they provided, albeit in the car park. Her father, who was in his nineties at the time, needed regular blood tests. He also had stomach problems. Instead of going into the surgery he was successfully examined in the car park, the car seat was tipped back, and the doctor examined him.

She did her parents shopping, as well as that of her neighbours. They were either elderly and/or vulnerable and were sheltering, so could not shop for themselves. She also walked dogs for various people and helped GOWNS who had over seventy people on their books.

During lockdown, one of her children contracted Covid. He remained in his bedroom while trays of food were taken up to him and any visits to the bathroom were thoroughly disinfected to avoid contamination. Luckily, the rest of the family remained negative.

Two of her adult children, living at home, were unable to go to work as one worked in hospitality and the other as a tattooist, but they were company for each.

The family did not know how long lockdown would last, so they created a routine and stuck to it. Each week, it included running or walking. It was easy to do as there are lots of walks around the village. Just walking through the village, everyone was friendly and spoke to each other from a distance.

One of the things in their routine was baking. For this, they went to the local supermarkets where they had to wait patiently in long queues. Although she found this annoying, she did find that generally people were very good. The frustrating thing was people panic buying. This meant Tesco did not always have some of the ingredients she wanted. Even so, the family tried to make the same meals for the same days each week, for instance she knew it was Thursday because they always had lasagne. All the local smaller shops in Bishops Cleeve continued to open, such as the butchers and Joyce Arnold (the grocer), which she found both helpful and very good. She felt it was a shame that the local shop had shut saying, 'it would have been a backbone of the village during lockdown,' but it was not to be.

Throughout April and May 2020, the weather was so good her family spent most of their time in their garden and even made a compost bin, as the rubbish tip had been closed, due to the pandemic.

Then there was VE Day. All the neighbours were out in their front gardens with their families. There were bunting and flags, some made tea and cakes while others had glasses of wine. It was a gloriously sunny day.

Once things began to get back to normal, her children like others, were able to go back to their jobs. They then found; they were rushed off their feet as everyone was making the most of their regained freedom. Despite this, they still appreciated being back at work.

The downside of lockdown for her family was that any booked holidays had to be deferred or cancelled, although it did give her time at home with her family, which she would miss.

Memory 5

They were able to go to Tesco, but visits were limited. Instead, they had to do a big shop rather than go every day. She felt the children were eating her and her husband out of house and home. The children continued to go to school and were kept in 'bubbles,' groups of children of mixed ages, as they were deemed 'key kids', in other words, children of key workers. This was because her husband was in the police. It had become apparent to Government that without key workers, society and the economy would grind to a halt.

Since the start of lockdown, the weather had been lovely, they enjoyed that period. They explored the local area and did a lot of geocaching. She explained that this was when people hide small treasures or notes on public footpaths or around the hills and fields for others to find. An example she gave was of a list of people who had been there before, once it had been found you could add your name to the list, then it was left for other people to find. It was also a lot safer for their children to ride their bikes as there was little or no traffic.

They were on the WhatsApp group for GOWNS and kept an eye on the elderly lady next door and joined in the 'Clap for the NHS,' every Thursday to show their support.

After lockdown, her younger child burst into tears when she was able to go back to school and see her friends, face to face again, but the older child had become anxious about going back to school. Although people were anxious, she felt everyone went back on their treadmills and back to their old routines. However, she said it was nice to see their family again and to realise what was important to them. It gave them time to rethink their priorities, and a change of career beckoned. She said, 'Lockdown made us take the decision to move away. It was an upheaval for the girls, but it gave us the confidence to make decisions that we might not have done otherwise.'

In hindsight, she felt it was a wonderful time in many ways, for instance, they appreciated the different pace of life and how quiet it became. There were lots of positive things about it.

Memory 6

She said she and her husband worked from home for the first time. It was something neither had done before, but it worked well. It was challenging but they did not need to furlough anyone.

Their children were sent home from school on the Friday before lockdown. Her Year 9 son was told he would have to do a mock exam for his Geology GCSE the following Friday. She felt he had no time to prepare as they had not even finished the syllabus! Both children continued their lessons at home. The school set the lessons, it was almost a full timetable, so the children worked every day until 3pm. All the after-school activities stopped overnight, although Brownies continued online. A family routine was quickly established which included the online PE sessions by Joe Wicks.

Even so, before a vaccination had been created, the more she read about Covid the more she decided it was better to avoid seeing anyone or go anywhere. Some of their relatives live in the village, but because they were older or had had recent operations or, like her, had an underlying condition, they, too, were 'shielding' to avoid unnecessary contact with others, so they could not see them anyway.

Food shopping went online. It was difficult to get slots even though they tried lots of different supermarkets. This was a particular problem for her as she had a medically restrictive diet. GOWNS offered them help, 'they were so good,' she said.

By Easter they were going on long walks to keep fit, for instance to Dixton and on to Winchcombe and back. They discovered all sorts of footpaths that they would never have known about otherwise. They also played lots of board and card games as a family and watched TV. She felt that 'the show must go on as normally as possible.'

For VE Day, everyone in the road sat in their front gardens or actually in the road, no-one was using their cars, so there was no fear of passing traffic. Everyone in their road had tea and cakes. It was quite sociable, although distanced.

They clapped for the NHS every Thursday and their son used the opportunity to play his drums. They also had hospital appointments, and these went ahead as usual, but the hospital seemed deserted, although she added, 'at least it was where we were.'

As things got better and less scary, places started to offer take-away services although some she tried did not come out as far as Gotherington.

Once lockdown was relaxed, they thought about holidays. At the end of July 2020, they were due to go on holiday in Northern Spain. They packed to go the following Tuesday, but on the Saturday, Spain locked down. Unperturbed, they looked at France but decided not to go there as the Covid figures were too high. That meant they had two weeks booked off work and although they got their money back, they had nowhere to go. She said by now they were going stir crazy. Luckily, they knew someone who had a house in the UK to which they could drive. Driving any distance was quite disconcerting. When the car went in for its annual service, it had only travelled 4000 miles! They had driven it so seldom.

Throughout the time, she felt life was at a lot slower pace, 'like our grandparents would have experienced all those years ago,' she said. The family saw and did a lot more together and she felt it was lucky that the weather was so good. She finished by saying, 'I wish the world would go into lockdown again once in a while.'

Memory 7

All the commitments in his diary were quickly cancelled. Initially, he felt very negative for the future, but believed there would be a vaccine eventually. He only did what he felt needed to be done without putting himself or his family at risk. He said he was incredibly grateful for all the help he received during lockdown.

He used Click and Collect for a variety of things, but the shortages in the supermarkets he found worrying. Instead, he went to the farm shop and Joyce Arnold, the greengrocer in Bishops Cleeve, for his fruit and vegetables.

He found that the lockdown seemed to 'pick up the pulse of nature', and he deliberately woke up at four in the morning to hear the dawn chorus. In the daytime, he also found it was so quiet except for the sounds of the village and Woolstone, which he enjoyed. There seemed lots of birdsong, the sounds of lambs in the fields and the dairy herd, even the sounds of children playing. He could hear people in their houses playing various instruments too. He felt there was an enormous musical talent in the village which was a real joy to him.

He was happy to walk down the middle of the road knowing there would be no traffic. It was also good to put names to faces. He felt incredibly lucky to live in Gotherington walking along and chatting to people while keeping a distance between them.

VE Day confirmed what he thought about the village. He had no idea what other villages or towns were doing but here people celebrated. He said, 'It was fantastic, I walked around and saw lots of people having picnics and raising a glass or two. It was a good excuse to do something different. I marched around in uniform as Lord Lieutenant, representing the Queen and sang happy birthday to someone.

He feels more positive now that lockdown has been eased, although he still tries not to listen to the news. He has seen more of his family recently than he had done for years. It was a particular joy that his son was able to come and stay.

After the first lockdown, during a relaxation period, he felt going into Cheltenham was uncomfortable, particularly walking along the pavements, wondering who would give way first. It was a new experience, judging people, probably wrongly he felt. The town felt like a different tribe to the village. 'Cheltenham has been really hit by this; it was as if someone had turned out the lights' he said.

He added, 'There was a kind of serenity to the time which allowed many people to reduce their stress and not to be carried along needlessly.' Having said that, he did not envy anyone who ran a business.

He found the experience not all that different from his normal life because of his lifestyle. He felt that everyone in the village were 'much of a muchness.'

Memory 8

This couple were regular church goers, but after lockdown was announced, the church went online. Several of their adult children, unlike them, had booked holidays that coincided with lockdown, but they were cancelled, and they got their money back.

The couple walked as much as possible, but they were wary of walking too much because of the Government restrictions. However, they did worry that the village buses would be cut due to lack of use once the pandemic was over. This, she said, would particularly affect the older residents. However, she did admit, that she would not want to take the bus because of the risk of catching Covid. Their daughter also shopped online for them rather than letting them shop for themselves.

They also helped in the community and found that many people in the village, who people think of as active, have hidden conditions which makes them vulnerable. GOWNS did a wonderful job but most of the members were of retirement age or were vulnerable, so Peter Barbour set up a younger WhatsApp group and GOWNS liaised with him. The church organised the DBS checks and insurance for the younger group. To find out who needed their help, they knocked on doors to get a better idea of who might need them.

The food distribution group operated through GOWNS. Lucy Barbour fronted the local deliveries and the couple helped take them to people's front doors. Waitrose gave away their fruit and vegetables too. This came to the Old Chapel and people took it for their neighbours. The Shutters Inn was also very generous and gave away the ingredients they had for the meals they could no longer provide.

It was nice getting to know people and sharing. Those on the new estate were particularly helpful. The couple thought it was triggered by their not being able to work. As things got better, people used GOWNS less, but it was also good for those who had become lonely and isolated.

All the couple's children began working from home but their son, in London, caught Covid and self-isolated. As their children did not want the couple to catch anything, they were cautious about visiting them. Their children organised a family WhatsApp group, which meant a lot to them. It was also their Golden Wedding Anniversary in the summer, so when things eased, they all came and celebrated in the garden while sitting well away from each other.

They thought lockdown had a big effect on their grandchildren who could not go to school. They were also sad that they had not been able to see as much of them as the couple would have liked. They said, 'We knew that Covid was not going away, so we had to get on with our lives, while abiding by the government rules, so we always used masks and kept our distance.' They also had to go to Gloucester Royal Hospital regularly and both felt that their treatment there was good.

They noticed during lockdown there was a sudden significant drop in the levels of traffic through the village and a subsequent increase of people riding bikes., although after lockdown, there was an immediate increase in car travel. They continued to walk as they did not think it was wise yet to take the bus, but added, 'even before lockdown it felt, at times, as if the bus was our own personal taxi service as so few people used it. Now, it is as if trust in the service has been damaged, and if people do not use it, it will be stopped.'

They found there were positives too, with lots of sharing of help and experience. There were boxes of toys and other things on people's drives that were being given away. It has been a strange year they concluded.

Memory 9: Gotherington Plant Nursery

They felt quite emotional listening to Boris' speech. They did not know what to expect but during lockdown, their other garden centre, Toddington Nursery's lease had come to an end and had closed, so everything was transferred to Gotherington. They said, 'We felt as if we were fighting to keep our business.'

They felt lucky that the weather was so good. The police and the council said they could open a 'Click and Collect' service, so they put ordered stock out on trollies, before they opened, and people came and collected them. They found they were very busy, 'it was full on 24-7, our feet never touched the ground right from the start. We had a minimum of a thousand emails a week. We felt we were serving a purpose, there were lots of deliveries and the public rallied round.' They were often exhausted, filling orders well into the evening, sometimes as late as nine or ten o'clock at night. It did not start calming down until mid-July.

Their daughters did the shopping, made the meals, and did the housework while their parents worked flat out in the plant nursery. They also had a couple of staff in their 70s but, luckily, they were able to keep them all.

They did not mix with other people but still clapped each Thursday to show their appreciation for everything the NHS were doing. They could hear others clapping as the sound drifted up from the main part of the village.

With parents in residential care, this was a worry. They were not allowed on the premises, but later they could visit, although this was conducted through an open window.

Strangely, during lockdown, they did not have a problem getting stock, but when they started to reopen after lockdown, they did. It was a stressful year.

Memory 10

Before the first lockdown, she worked three days a week and her girls went to the local school. She also took them to the many clubs available in the evenings and ran the Brownie Pack in the village hall once a week, then at the weekend, she caught up with friends.

Instead, during lockdown, each week the family did online quizzes with friends and craft activities for Brownies on Zoom. She had good feedback from parents and for many it became part of their routine.

Once lockdown was announced, the school closed, and her children had worksheets. They did two to three hours schoolwork a day. She felt it also helped that one parent was able to work mainly from home. She found it quite refreshing to stay at home during lockdown and not rush about.

However, as a Community Physiotherapist, she could be called out to anywhere in Gloucestershire. She carried full personal protection equipment (PPE) and had to balance face to face or videos sessions with deciding whether people were cognitively intact or not. Also, as she worked for the NHS, she felt she should not clap each Thursday evening, when everyone else showed their appreciation for NHS workers. Instead, her children drew lots of rainbows which signified the family's appreciation.

Superstores, like Sainsburys, allowed NHS workers to shop an hour before everyone else, but it was limited to one person rather than the whole family. Even so, the shops sometimes ran out of items, such as flour. For those that could not shop for themselves, she and her husband helped with GOWNS dropping things off.

Their girls played safely outside as there was no traffic and did the Guide's challenges too, such as teddies in the windows around the village. The dog was happier too as they were all at home and they went for longer walks. They also all sat down for meals together, something they had not always been able to do before. Then for VE Day, they had a picnic on their driveway.

She felt as though she had not seen people face to face for ages.

Memory 11

Initially the couple thought 'what do we do now?'. All the social side of their lives went, which particularly affected his golfing life. They could not even go to see their family and they did not live very far away.

They were deemed vulnerable and felt any choice was taken away from them making them depend on others. Their daughter said they should let someone else do the shopping, but the couple wanted to do their own and wanted to remain independent. Even so, their daughter insisted, and their son-in-law did the shopping for them. When they were able to shop for themselves again, they were pleased to see that Tesco had introduced a one-way system.

They felt that the village was friendly, and their neighbours offered to help if they needed it. Instead of going out, they spent most of their time in the garden. The good weather helped. During this time, the couple had two birthdays, but the family did not come into the house and only came to the door to drop things off.

By September, the Gardening Club were proposing meeting, but they were still not keen to meet in any enclosed environment.

They felt they did not travel anywhere before lockdown, so it made no real difference to their way of life, although they were particularly worried about the impact lockdown had on their young granddaughter.

Memory 12

This person was a teacher. Her secondary school quickly closed after the government announced its lockdown measures. It meant that as a teacher, she had to give lessons via video link, mark homework, which she did in the evenings, and home school her own children. She said it was nice not to have to worry about the children getting out of the house in time to go to school.

She found shopping difficult because some of the supermarket shelves were cleared of the strangest things. She commented, 'it was laughable.' One thing she did run out of was flour. Even so, the next day, someone had put some underneath the car for her to use. Although she was not involved in GOWNS, she also took some vegetables round to the elderly lady who lived on her own by the shop.

Even though both sides of the couple's parents did not live locally, they stuck to the rules and did not visit them. Instead, she remembered quiet evenings, walks with the dog, running and cycling and exercising to Joe Wicks. The family have lots of interests and Beavers online kept her children going with various tasks and badges as rewards. They also took round pebbles with rainbows on them and dropped them off anonymously at various doorsteps to show their support for the NHS.

The weather helped too, so her and her husband dug out the large 'pots' at the side of their garden. Gotherington History Society had researched into them as they seemed a strange thing to have at the side of the house and told her that they were old cesspits!

On VE Day, the children made some bunting and they all sat outside and chatted to the neighbours across the road. It was nice to have company.

She liked the slow pace of life. She did not have to rush and did not feel she missed out on anything. It was a lifestyle that she felt suited her.

Memory 13

Before lockdown he was living in Gloucester as he had let his house in Gotherington and was waiting for the tenants to move out. He intended only to be in the village for the winter and then go back to Australia. This had become quite a routine for him. Instead, he had to stay in Gotherington for the duration of lockdown.

He got up with the sunrise and jogged round the playing field, so he did not meet anyone. He also sorted out the garden and did any DIY in the house that was needed which he admitted he may not have done otherwise.

In September 2020, he had some friends who died from Covid and went to five funerals. He thinks there will be several years of Covid before us.

Memory 14

Government and doctors gave advice, which she and her husband followed, but she felt at the beginning of the pandemic, the only person you could count on was yourself. She did not feel Covid would go away until there was a vaccine.

The family business, before lockdown, was always stressful as people did not seem to have any patience and the work took time. Once lockdown was announced, life was less stressful than they thought. There was no choice, so they just had to accept it and stop. She said the Government grants helped the business, but they were in a 'good place' anyway. When everything stopped, they painted the house from top to bottom as they already had a lot of paint.

Not being able to see their children and grandchildren was difficult. Their children were in Florida before lockdown was announced but by the beginning of March, all the theme parks there were closing or had closed. Their children managed to get earlier flights so that they got back to the UK before everything here locked down. She and her husband had been expecting to go to America too, but they deferred it. Later in the year, they were going to go to France, but they decided against that as well.

She went shopping very early in the morning and felt that lockdown made her plan her meals, unlike before when she used to pop to the shops whenever she felt like it. They had quiet evenings in, walked the dog, went running and cycling and exercised to Joe Wicks online.

Further afield, she was grateful that her brother had a granny flat next to his house and was able to look after their mother. However, during lockdown, her mother fell over and needed respite care. It was difficult to get her in anywhere, although eventually her brother was able to, but she described it as 'hell on Earth' trying to find somewhere.

Looking back in the summer of 2020, she said it has been a nice break, although we did drink more than usual. They felt they connected more with our neighbours generally and particularly on VE Day when they placed two wine glasses in the centre of the road and the couple across the road, did the same. Then they took it in turns to fill the glasses with wine. At one stage, there were four glasses, two with white wine and two with red wine in the middle of the road. They listened out for any traffic, but they did not expect any as under lockdown rules, with certain exceptions, no one was allowed to drive anywhere so it wasn't a problem, and none came. Later, they walked around the village and had socially distanced chats.

'The village had a real community spirit. It was really nice and relaxing. Now that lockdown seems to have ended, people are more pleasant and accepting,' she said.

Memory 15

Another family with their own business had to furlough their staff from the start of lockdown.

Two of their sons came back from university. One son was in his final year so had to finish his dissertation while he was at home. Luckily, their two boys were company for each and did things together during their unexpected time at home.

The family did their own shopping and dropped letters round to their neighbours to ask them if they needed them to shop for them as well.

Seeing a dentist though was a problem as they were all closed. Instead, when her husband wanted to go to the dentist, he was only able to get a prescription for antibiotics rather than being seen. Luckily, this did the trick.

They developed their own routine and did more walking all of which she loved. There was no fear of missing out, 'why race around?' she said.

After lockdown, she was choosier as to how she spends her time and was more reflective.

Memory 16

'We knew Italy and Spain were having problems and as London is an international hub, it was obvious it would happen here too, but we never thought it would get that bad', she said.

Every week they would normally have played Bridge, gone to the Gardening Club monthly and Film Club whenever there was a film they wanted to see. They would socialise with friends, both locally and elsewhere too, but when lockdown was announced, it all stopped.

They had intended to go to America, but that was cancelled. Instead, they thought they would go to France, but as it got closer to the time, they realised they could not go there either. The couple had plans for their whole family to come for their fiftieth wedding anniversary, but they were unable to visit, as government rules were not to travel, with only a few exceptions.

Her father died in June; he was 96. At that time, only 30 people were able to attend the crematorium and there could be no wake afterwards. A resident in the village also died. She had fallen and was taken to Cheltenham Hospital where it was believed she contracted Covid. She had lived in the village a long time and was well known. The hearse came slowly along The Lawns and paused outside her house before it went off to Cheltenham and the crematorium. This happened to others in the village too.

Her face-to-face appointment at the Nuffield Hospital was cancelled so she had a telephone consultation instead. She and her husband also received an NHS letter telling them to shield, so they did, spending their time in the garden and house.

Having to 'shield' caused difficulties as she was a member of GOWNS and, like her, many of the volunteers were older and isolating. Despite this, they still had lots of telephone calls for their help, although they felt they could not help anyone.

Lucy Barber in the village stepped in to save the day. She asked for volunteers who were not classed as vulnerable. These people were younger and 40 came forward. They kept the GOWNS phone number and set up a team in a WhatsApp group. The church covered the insurance, and they were all DBS checked. If anyone needed anything, they could 'phone and the WhatsApp Team would do it. When they collected any shopping, the payment for the goods could be left in an envelope on the doorstep or paid direct via bank transfer to the organiser who would then reimburse whoever bought the shopping. The delivery was all free. Waitrose said they would deliver free perishable food and the WhatsApp Team collected it from the Old Chapel and delivered it to those who needed it. 'They were brilliant!', she said.

During lockdown, she improved her IT skills and used Zoom to keep in touch with family and friends. The couple were able to order their shopping online and had it delivered. People quickly realised that they too could get an online supermarket delivery slot, so to book a slot, they had to stay up until midnight just to get one.

The independent shops, like the Farm Shop down Stoke Road, did Click and Collect. They had lots of fresh fruit and vegetables. The only problem was that, for a time, it was impossible to get flour from the supermarkets. There was a shortage of toilet paper in some of the shops too, but if her husband went to Lidl rather than Tesco, he was able to buy as much toilet paper as he wanted. Gotherington Plant Nursery was very good. They sold their plants via Click and Collect too and when anything was delivered, masks were worn.

By the summer of 2020, lockdown was relaxed, and the couple began driving a little bit further afield and walked around Stow on the Wold and Morton in Marsh where there is little chance of seeing anyone. Even so, they still wore masks and gloves. They also started to go into shops, but they did not have pub lunches.

She was also a Trustee of the Old Chapel. It lost its income overnight, but luckily it was planned to be closed for several months to be renovated, so it did not really matter anyway. Then, over the summer when people were able to go about their businesses again, the repairs and refurbishment went ahead, and it finished on time.

She felt things were not really going to go back to normal though.

Memory 17

Before lockdown, he walked long distances with a walking group. This stopped with lockdown and so he walked locally on his own instead. He also regularly visited Nature In Art, near Gloucester, but that too closed, as did Slimbridge Wetland Centre where he went as a regular bird watcher.

He and his wife's families do not live locally so he missed regular contact with them. Modern technology overcame this, and they took part in regular family quizzes.

The dynamics of lockdown made them feel besieged. They had been avid holiday takers and a couple of the holidays they had expected to take were cancelled or postponed. They missed taking them but were happy when they got their money back. Once lockdown started to lift, he wanted to start booking holidays again, but his wife was more apprehensive and felt they should wait.

He is a trustee for the Old Chapel which closed and so did The Church Luncheon Club which left many older people without company and lonely. A few of the older ladies got quite depressed. It hit some people quite hard.

It also meant a loss of income for the Old Chapel. The Trustees were supposed to be getting Gilder and Snape, local firms, to renovate the Old Chapel but lockdown prevented it. Initially he thought; "'oh bugger,' we can't do anything, but it gives us something to think about."

Even with the relaxation of the rules, it has had a continuing impact on the Old Chapel. There were rules limiting the number of people who could attend clubs inside the building. Even then, he said 'people would only do what they feel comfortable with.'

He also appreciated the work of the NHS and their diligent approach throughout lockdown. For him, VE Day and seeing Edward Gillespie (below) walking round the village in his Lord Lieutenant uniform was one of the highlights.

He thought that lockdown did not impact too much on the village and that everyone had to learn to live with it, saying 'Things are definitely improving now, although the nation has suffered quite badly, it has been a bit of a roller coaster and the after taste will linger for some time. I'm an optimist so I'm sure things will get better.'

Memory 18

During the first few days, she spent her time gardening and watching the birds. She found a nest of chicks and enjoyed watching the mother bird feeding them.

GOWNS sent her a leaflet saying they would help her if she needed it. She has family in the village, and they did her shopping and anything else she needed, but she was still grateful GOWNS were there if she had needed them.

The VE Day celebrations, she thought, were lovely and everyone was very friendly. It was her birthday, which in 1945 she remembered clearly and wrote this note:

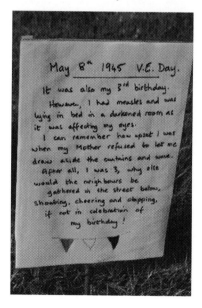

Everyone at that end of the village sang 'happy birthday,' including the Queen's representative Edward Gillespie, who saluted her wearing full uniform.

By the time lockdown ended, she said she was fed up with the whole thing. It was nice to see the pub open again in the summer and a little bit of normality return. It was a relief to see her family again as she had not been able to see them during the months of lockdown, and as she said, 'they only live up the road!'

Memory 19

She felt it was lucky that the weather in the spring and summer had been so good. She kept busy with her dogs and gardening. It gave her the opportunity to spring clean and redesign her garden. She also noticed the children around the village were able to put their tents up in their gardens and play outside. She did lots of crafts, such as felting, cross stitching, making soap, knitting and cards and read several books. Company was not a problem either, as she was able to talk to her next-door neighbours, albeit over the fence, and she got a kitten which helped too. Her youngest son did her shopping online every week and the delivery she found was free!

She, like most of the people in the village, clapped for the NHS and said, 'it was lovely to see the people in the pub come outside and clap too.' She was glad not to be ill though. 'I was scared of going into hospital.' There was a death in the village, people came out of their houses as the hearse drove slowly by. It was sad, not only because of the death but also because only a few people could attend the funeral as numbers were so limited.

She finished saying, 'We are very lucky to live round here.'

Memory 20

One family's daughter, like all children, had to stay at home. The routine of face-to-face lessons in primary, secondary and special schools stopped during lockdown. Another daughter, who taught in a secondary school had to give her lessons online. Like all families, those living away were not able to visit. Instead, they used Facetime and the internet to keep in touch with their friends and family.

From the start of the lockdown, the mother of the family became a voluntary responder for the NHS. She had to undertake training and upload various documents to prove who she was before she was allowed to take calls.

In March, her father died. Luckily, she had seen him before lockdown but sadly, as her parents did not live locally, and numbers were restricted, this meant the family was not allowed to go to the funeral, which was particularly difficult for her mother.

The family adopted a cat, whom she described as 'a work in progress and frightened of everything!' The family also did jigsaws, artwork, crosswords, learned to crochet, and read a lot as well as going for long walks.

The family did their food shopping online and used Amazon too for other purchases. In the early days, everyone wanted to make bread, but flour became difficult to buy, so as she had a lot, she gave others her flour and yeast and made bread for her neighbours and friends with what she had left.

She felt that the lockdown period was an attitude of mind, saying 'we just got on with it.'

Memory 21

The local clubs stopped, and the walking clubs brought in a lot of regulations, so they hardly walked at all. Their grandchildren were sent home from school and the school itself closed quite soon after. Both their daughter and grandchildren were ill at the start of lockdown. Their daughter isolated for six weeks, although at that stage they could not say it was Covid. Lockdown meant that all visiting, and socialising stopped so, because the weather was good, the couple did a lot of gardening instead.

The couple usually helped run the food bank in Bishops Cleeve, which is part of North Cotswolds Food Bank, and run from St Michael's Centre, Church Road. Tesco, in Bishops Cleeve, supports it, the shop in the village was also a collection point. The local WI and the vicar knew about it too. The food bank caters for all sorts of people as poverty is often hidden and with layoffs and furloughs, this was likely to create new clients. There was also a five week wait for universal credit, so the

Food Bank steps in. With lockdown, the whole system had to reorganise. For instance, it could no longer go door to door. Over lockdown, those on free school meals were also given vouchers to help their families. However, the couple found, like many of the helpers, because they were older and had to isolate, so they could no longer help the Trust.

They also noticed that people had begun to panic buy. They found that for a couple of weeks, the shelves were a 'bit lean for fresh stuff'. Tesco cut down on the number of items people could buy to try and stop this. At one stage, people could only buy three carrots at a time!

Later, Waitrose donated some fruit and vegetables to the village, leaving it at the Old Chapel. The Shutters too gave away all their perishable goods. The couple said, 'Ellen Cook and her husband Adrian, did a great job of organising it all.'

Memory 22

She works for a surgery. She found there were lots of changes and lots of phone calls. The 111 service, and not the doctors, dealt with people with symptoms that could be Covid. There was no Reception, and the doors were locked. Instead, all the appointments were organised by telephone. Once the personal protection equipment (PPE) was sorted out, the doctors or nurses could see patients either in the surgery or in the car park. The doctors were not seeing people face-to-face for routine things. Instead, they relied on videos and photos. It changed the way the practice worked. She does not think the surgery will go back to the way they were.

She worked from home and continued to do so, which meant there was not much social contact. Her husband was working from home anyway, so he continued to have lots of Zoom meetings. Her son, however, worked shifts in a large store in Cheltenham and although he did not lose his job, he was furloughed. When he went back, he found there were lots of arguments from people not wanting to queue and not wanting to pay by card.

Her other son was at university. At the start of the lockdown, the university told them all to pack up and go home. The university was very good since it repaid the rent of all the university tenants, some of which were still living in the flats. Her son came home, but unfortunately, he could not visit his girlfriend as she lived in another part of the country and extended travel was restricted to local travel only and only if absolutely necessary.

The family cancelled their holidays and were unable to go to concerts or visit the National Trust which closed as well. The big change, she felt, was not to be able to see people who lived far away, such as extended family. Her sister and family live in Wales, where she said the rules were stricter than the English ones, but they stuck to them as neither the English nor Welsh families wanted to break them. Instead, they used Zoom to keep in touch.

Before lockdown, they usually had family weekends together and she missed those, as well as seeing friends. She missed 'giving and receiving hugs.' She felt that as a family, being unable to see anyone, they had to rely on their own household which made them feel closer.

Having extra adults at home though meant the food bill rose. Prior to Covid, she did all her shopping online but once it hit, all the slots went even though she was a regular customer. It was difficult to keep on top of shopping online although eventually, she was given priority shopping slot because she worked for the NHS.

Her husband walked the dog up on Cleeve Common until that too closed. Then, walks were village based only and they missed long walks and going to a pub for drinks afterwards.

They did a lot more gardening, more than they had done in other years. They ordered a greenhouse at the beginning of April but had to wait for it as the company had sold out. When it did arrive, they grew seeds; it was very successful.

Once the rules were relaxed a little, they began cycling and went further afield. She cycled across the Evesham Road down towards Springfield Kennels. Her ride was, she said, 'really quiet, there were no cars and no planes either, it was really nice.'

Sometime later when the rules were relaxed a little, she went into town and was shocked to see everyone wearing masks and how sociable people were, as if they were immune. It put her off going into town. She also remembered having her first ice cream, saying, 'it was bliss and something I had not made myself.'

She was happier that they had come through it. 'I had had enough. I was so glad that it happened in the Spring and Summer when the weather was so nice, and we were able to spend a lot of time outdoors. I cleared the plants off the war memorial later than usual, it was nice to do something that felt more normal. We saved a lot of money too during lockdown as we could not go anywhere and did not want to buy anything either.'

Memory 23: Postman

He was busier than normal. All postmen and women were classed as key workers so did not have to isolate. He found that people went online and ordered a variety of things as they were no longer able to go out and buy them in actual shops. This meant there was a large increase in the volume of parcels and packages coming through the Post Office Depot in Cheltenham. There were so many that the Post Office had to take on extra postmen and women to deliver them.

Memory 24: Dairy Farmer

He felt that 2020 was no different for him than in other years. He just carried on as usual.

Memory 25: Agricultural Farmer

She felt that 2020 did not affect her family very much either.

Memory 26: Springfield Kennels

Their business, like other businesses, was affected by the pandemic. The kennels were still open for animals that needed grooming for health reasons, but the public appeared not to know this. The telephone continued to ring as owners rang to cancel bookings. 'It was soul destroying.' The boarding kennel was empty, apart from those unable to pick up their pets because they were unable to come back to the UK from abroad.

Staff were furloughed and Government grants applied for but the utility bills etc still had to be paid. Even during the time between lockdowns, when many could go on holiday, people decided to take a 'staycation', so did not need to board their dog or cat.

Once things began to get less restrictive, the kennels opened, but few used it as people were unaware that they could put their dogs and cats into their kennels and cattery.

Before the second lockdown, they decided to go on holiday and used what was known as an 'air corridor.'

They took their campervan through the Channel Tunnel and without stopping drove through France to Germany. France, at this time, was a 'red' country. This meant it was on a list that people could not visit for a holiday. Germany, however, was on a 'green' list so people could holiday there. From there, they went on to Italy where they found no tourists and had a wonderful time.

Memory 27

The couple felt that they were not affected adversely as they do not go out much anyway. Instead, they passed the time making up themed quizzes and games for the younger members of their family, who do not live close to them. He wrote stories for them called Percy the Pigeon and the children sent back pictures of themselves with pigeons. After each chapter, he asked what they thought would happen next then wrote another part of the story. He also wrote a story called Charlie Larkin based loosely on his childhood escapades. The children loved hearing their mother read them.

Like others, the couple used Ancestry to trace their ancestors and were able to get back to the 17th century. They also enjoyed using photographs to make up family albums.

Memory 28

This retired head teacher, living by herself, found her overriding memory was one of loneliness and she knew that the Vicar worried about her. She was amazed at the number of people who offered her help in their different ways. The Vicar's wife did her shopping, and she even had a birthday present delivered to her door. The newspapers and milk were delivered as usual, so she felt that she did not need the help of GOWNS as everything was already organised.

For the first month, she barely went out but as time went on, she went for short walks down into the village. Once a cyclist, possibly a previous pupil, went past and said good morning to her using her name, which amused her as she had not taught for some time. She found everyone very friendly. She clapped for the NHS and saw more of her neighbours then than at any other time.

Once things began to relax a little, her cleaner rang to ask her if she wanted her to resume cleaning and she did. Her cleaner had not been able to come for the duration of lockdown. It was not until Christmas however, that she was able to see her friends in Bishops Cleeve.

She found, as things began to become more normal, she wanted to go further afield, but her car would not start. She felt this was due to lack of use. She rang the AA who came immediately, but the man had to push it out of the garage before he could do anything to it. Once it was going again, she drove all the way to Gretton. She felt strange doing it but by the time she came back to Gotherington driving had become normal practice again.

She was glad that she had a computer as even church services had to go online.

Memory 29: Reverend Richard Reakes

Reverend Richard Reakes was the Team Vicar for the churches of Bishops Cleeve, Woolstone, Oxenton and Southam, all of which were in the benefice of Bishops Cleeve.

In the first week of lockdown, all places of worship closed and the churches at Woolstone and Oxenton were locked, even cutting the grass around the churches and graves was suspended. He thought it had never happened before.

Reverend Reakes had copies of the members of each church and checked their addresses against the electoral role. Instead of attending church, he rang all his parishioners every week. He found this was good because he could have a proper conversation with his parishioners. It was a useful way of keeping in touch with those that wanted him to. It only stopped when he was able to visit people again.

A video link was also set up for those on the internet. People could then choose to watch it or not. Initially, there were 50 people viewing his sermons, but as time went on, other people got in touch and eventually people as far as India, New Zealand and Australia were viewing them. In lockdown, the church was reaching more people than those who attended the church face-to-face. It made people feel more connected. He said the downside of lockdown was that those who did not have the internet felt more isolated. Even though there were lots of positives during lockdown, the big thing that everyone seemed to miss was being with one another.

There were a few funerals in Gotherington and people stood on the street as a hearse slowly passed by. This was not his doing, he said, 'it just happened.' Then, when the coffin arrived for burial, a short service was held round the graveside with only 30 people, which, at the time, was the maximum number that could be present. One solution could be to hold a memorial service in the future, which might be helpful for families, but if the funeral was a long time ago, people might not want to. He said the situation was all very sad.

Baptisms and weddings were cancelled. Then, when these were allowed to go ahead, the numbers attending baptisms and weddings, including the bride and groom, was 30. It was a very sad time because people want their friends and family around them. He was concerned about the long-term effect this would have on people.

Even when the rules were relaxed in the summer, Evening Prayers were still held on Zoom. It was particularly isolating for those that did not feel confident about coming back to church. Once services began again, there were directives to which the church had to adhere. All Orders of Service had to be quarantined for

72 hours after their use and the Church Warden's hands had to be sanitised before they could put them on the seats. The Parish Magazine also stopped as the rules kept changing and the editor was afraid that it might be publishing out of date information and telling people irrelevant things.

Lockdown curbed everyone's freedom and Reverand Reakes felt it would take its toll. 'Young people want to be with their friends, social interaction is very important,' he said.

The Vicar felt that GOWNS did a marvellous job. Most of the people in GOWNS were over 70 and had to isolate, so instead, a group of younger people networked and after a while they worked with GOWNS. They established a group to do the work of GOWNS. The church sorted out the safeguarding certificates and it was soon up and running. It helped that many younger people had to work from home so had time to help.

Unfortunately, Remembrance Day in November did not take place. He clapped for the NHS which he felt this really brought the community together. He took long walks and cycled, hardly ever seeing a car. There was a sense of tranquillity and peace.

He also considered the months ahead in 2020. He thought that in December, in the run up to Christmas, there may be carols at the bottom of the garden, but Christingle is unlikely to happen, neither is the Crib

Service at Woolstone, the Village Hall carol service nor the midnight service. (They did not take place that year).

He felt that even if they did not go ahead, the rhythm of the year was very important. That it was subconscious thing. The danger is that people will not want to organise anything or take risks.

He felt that everyone had to abide by the rules and should continue to do so, because rather than coming to an end, this might be only the middle of the pandemic. 'When it is over it, will be good to look back and reflect, the rat race cannot carry on,' he said.

Memory 30: Church warden

When lockdown was announced in early March, the Parochial Church Council said that all the churches had to be closed and locked. The Vicar was also stopped from taking Holy Communion to private houses or to visit parishioners, nor could people go into the churches for a private moment of reflection and the bells were silent. No-one was allowed inside the church.

There were no baptisms or weddings and only open-air funerals as the coffins were not allowed to enter the church. There was an open-air funeral at Woolstone St. Martin De Tour, Church for Mr Wilson and there were open-air memorial services for others too.

At the height of the pandemic, all services were held on Zoom. The vicar held an evening prayer service once a week and a morning Sunday service every week. There were no Easter services in either 2020 or 2021 and no formal Remembrance Service although people got busy with their knitting needles and decked the church yards outside both Woolstone and Oxenton churches with red knitted poppies.

The Christmas Service in Woolstone Church did not take place, in 2020. The number of children with Covid was a particular worry so the Crib Service did not go ahead either. The church did not open again until October 2021.

At Oxenton, St John the Baptist Church as with Woolstone, it did not have a Christmas service in 2020 and no Easter service in either 2020 or 2021. St John the Baptist Church opened earlier than St Martin de Tour Church, in August 2021. Even so, where people could sit was marked out and their names and addresses taken in case, they found they later had Covid.

Memory 31

His family live in London and in Cheltenham. Despite some being quite close, he was not able to see them or his friends.

Covid did not make a lot of difference to his lifestyle. He was able to continue with his research. He looked after the house, read, and listened to the radio. He felt he had to spend a lot more time on his own, but it did not really stop him from doing anything he wanted to do.

He was aware of the support on offer and the deliveries around the village. It was good to know it was out there if it was needed, but he had no need for support and continued to shop for himself. He knew the times to go and when it was best not to, so he avoided those times. Occasionally he had to queue, but he did not mind doing that. He noticed shortages to begin with, but they were soon sorted out. It was not a problem, and he felt he could always go elsewhere.

He believed the NHS had not really been supported and did not really approve of clapping for the NHS as he felt it did not seem appropriate. He felt it was not clear who it was for, adding maybe it was just to make people feel better.

He noticed Covid had made a big impact on the village. He felt that a climate of fear had been created and that it had more psychological impact than actual impact on people.

The local VE Day celebrations passed him by and he was not aware of them. He noted that not only was there no Topics available, neither were there Parish Council minutes. He believed the Parish Council stopped meeting and was not clear why. He felt lockdown had only had a modest impact on his life.

Memory 32

He and his wife have lived in the village for over fifty years. They were aboard in March 2020 and were worried that they might be stranded if they delayed their departure, so they flew back before lockdown. The stewardesses on board the aeroplane all wore masks. Two ladies on the flight were hard of hearing, so the cabin staff had to take their masks off when they spoke to them so the ladies could lip read, which amused him.

He found lockdown was more dramatic than he had expected. All the clubs stopped, and the speakers had to be told that the village hall was locked and that their talks were cancelled. He and his wife had expected to visit places and meet up with family in the summer, but they were unable to do so.

Their adult children advised them to shop online, but they found it difficult. Instead, they went early to avoid the queues which were long and stretched right round the car park. They found that lunchtimes were a good time to go as it was less busy. They also felt Waitrose was good as the aisles were wider than some supermarkets. However, they could not go in as a couple from the same household, in any of the supermarkets but only one at a time.

Joyce Arnold Groceries in Bishops Cleeve was open throughout lockdown which was good. Tesco ran out of eggs, but Joyce Arnold always had them. Getting flour, was also a problem, particularly as they made their own bread. To remedy this, they cycled to Stanway Flour Mill and bought flour there instead of trying to get it at the supermarkets, although they tried to shop locally as much as they could.

They did not need GOWNS or the delivery of fresh food from the Old Chapel, but it was nice to know they could access help if they needed it. They also clapped for the NHS and were clapping for others as well, such as Joyce Arnold.

He had to go to hospital during the first lockdown. The ambulance paramedics were wonderful and very reassuring. Before Covid, they would have gone to Gloucester Royal Hospital, but instead his appointments were in Cheltenham Hospital. In the hospital, the first thing they did was a Covid test, before each appointment.

He also broke a tooth and rang the dentist for help. The dentist asked if it was painful. As it was not, they just put him on a list and did not do anything until after lockdown. Once lockdown had finished, the dentist saw him straight away.

The couple's hair grew, as all the hairdressers and barbers were closed. He did not like his new appearance. It did not matter that they were not going anywhere, once he was able to go out and barbers were open again, he had his hair cut.

The weather was good, so everything grew, though at times it was windy and when it was, all their sunflowers blew down. They expressed their thankfulness that they had a garden, as they could just go and lose themselves in it, unlike those living in the city.

They walked miles but they did not cycle far because they felt that people would be funny about it if they did. Also, they thought that if they took the car out and it broke down and they had to call a breakdown service, that would be difficult too, so they hardly drove anywhere unless it was for food shopping. Throughout the lockdown, they kept to the rules as they were supposed to be for everyone irrespective of where they lived, he noted.

The worst thing about lockdown for them was not being able to see their grandchildren. They missed them terribly particularly not being able to give them a hug, even though they spoke to them every day. One lot of grandchildren lived in Bromsgrove, which was not very

far away. When things got a bit better, they were able to visit them, even so, they did not go in the house and stayed instead in the garden. Their other grandchildren lived in Edinburgh and their lockdown went on longer, as Scotland was stricter than England. This meant even though the English lockdown rules were relaxed, they still could not go and see them.

Like many others in Gotherington, on VE Day, they put out a table and chairs and had tea and cake. It was a lovely hot day. All their neighbours came out and, like them, they walked around the village. There was bunting strung out across the hedges and a flag hanging from the upstairs window of one house. He said, 'it really was a jolly affair, even if the plan had been to have something on the playing field, it could not have been better.'

In lockdown, it was simple, every day was the same. They were never bored. They read a lot and she knitted a lot. They saved money as they never went anywhere or did anything. The pound went down and so did the cost of petrol, so they made sure the tank was full. Petrol prices were good for lorry drivers who did their best to keep delivering.

One thing he did not like was wearing a mask as he felt that his ears were too small to cope with a hearing aid, glasses, and a mask, but he wore one anyway.

One thing he was concerned about was that no-one was using the buses and that the buses going through the village would stop running, further isolating those without a car.

Memory 33

This family had both boys at university. Once lockdown, was announced the boys came home. The older one was unsure whether to stay at university or not but eventually he came home too. As his mother said, 'She did not want him stuck there.'

Her husband worked from home anyway so there was no change there. He was disabled, and so the carers came in every day despite lockdown. She was concerned about contamination, but she could not do everything for him and, as his wife, neither of them would want her to.

Her mother, who only lived in the next village, was not well. She was not in a 'home' but in her own house. The vicar regularly said prayers over the telephone for her. She said, 'He was excellent!' She went with her mother to all her appointments including to Gloucester Royal Hospital. Sadly, her mother died. They were only allowed a small funeral at the crematorium in Prestbury. She said that strangely, sorting out her mum's things helped during that time.

The family also stopped listening to The News as they felt that the rules were 'foggy'. She was worried about going to Tesco too. 'They were fantastic though', she said. There were clean trollies and one queue in and one queue out and a two-metre rule in place. 'They did a really good job.' The small local shops, like Joyce Arnold and Dave the Butcher 'were fantastic too.'

There were shortages of some foods, like rice, and a lot of things were pre-packaged rather than loose, which meant they were more than she needed. Luckily, she was able to swap some things with her sister, but she still noticed that her food bills went up. When she got back from the shops, she threw her mask and gloves away and washed her clothes in case they were contaminated. After lockdown, when she went to Marks and Spencer's food department, she felt like a child in a sweet shop!

The neighbours were all helpful and there was no need to ask GOWNS for anything. Like others, she clapped for the NHS and felt guilty when she did not. It was nice to see everyone clapping and making a noise. She went running, walking and dog walking. On VE Day, she said, 'We sat outside, it was lovely chatting with neighbours.'

After lockdown, she was very cautious and did not do a lot of things and only met up with friends in the park or the garden rather than inside. They also decided not to go away on holiday for a while.

Memory 34

She was self-employed so that meant after lockdown was announced, she put some of her sessions online and the two youngest children helped with the online music sessions as she could no longer meet groups face-to-face. The government gave grants for the self-employed so that was helpful. Her husband began working from home too.

Four days a week, she had left at nine o'clock in the morning to take pre-school music groups, after which she had to get back in time for the end of school and her own children, one of which had started secondary school; the others were still in Gotherington Primary School. After lockdown was announced, her children stopped going to school.

For a while, they did not worry about school and did some DIY instead, but lockdown went on and so they began home schooling. School started sending things home for the children. Initially the lessons were done half-heartedly, then the family started taking them more seriously. They set up a new routine, 9-9:30 am they started schoolwork. The younger one stopped at eleven and the older one at twelve. She rang a bell so that they knew it was time to stop, but they decided to be flexible when necessary. Two of them enjoyed their schoolwork and it was not a problem but the other one needed her to sit with him to get it done.

With the older family, they had Zoom sessions. She thought they probably did too much at the beginning and even did scavenger hunts via Zoom. In fact, they saw more of their family that way than they usually did face to face. They tried to make sure they were all alright. They were due to go to see their Irish family, but that was cancelled.

She felt shopping was a bit scary to begin with, so her husband did it. She was nervous about going out and touching something and accidently touching her face. Slowly she became more confident, and they shared the shopping. She enjoyed shopping at Tesco and the one-way system.

They clapped for the NHS, put up posters and communicated on Facebook. On the 8th May, we had VE Day. She said she 'plastered' the village with posters for it. People came out and had tea and cakes. It was nice to talk to neighbours across the gardens.

Lockdown for the family 'felt like a life of Riley!' They went for walks every day, even the teenager came with them and there were no arguments about it. The children did not leave the village for three months.

She felt better than before lockdown; it was for them an enforced sabbatical.

Memory 35: Garden House Nursery

In March, when lockdown hit, like the primary school the nursery school had to close immediately. No-one had expected lockdown to last for so long. The first lockdown lasted for six months from March to September.

Many parents had to work from home and had to keep their children with them. That meant that the nursery school had no income either from the nursery itself or from the After School Club. Despite this, like everyone else, they still had rent and bills to pay. This caused problems for some time. Like many of the children's parents, staff were furloughed, so although the government supported staff costs, it did not support the rent and other bills. Also, if staff were still working, for instance on paperwork, albeit without the children, they could not be furloughed.

The owners of the nursery school also had to re-register which added to extra stress. One member of staff was undergoing cancer treatment and given that no-one wanted to go to hospital with the threat of Covid hanging over the building, this too made life very stressful.

Looking back, both women felt, despite the stress and problems in 2020, the parents were very supportive and flexible and understood when some of the staff could not work, or the number of open days had to be cut. They were, however, glad when it was over.

Memory 36

Being a teacher at a boarding school, he had to keep working despite lockdown. He felt he was always on call, which he found difficult. His was a full day of teaching online, which had its positive points as there were no interruptions. It was very productive which meant there was a lot of marking, so from that point of view it hardly changed, he said. However, the children did not have face to face contact so there was no peer-to-peer social interaction.

At Easter, no internal exams took place. He felt that the 16- to 18-year-olds were a lost generation and that their first hurdles in life, such as interviews, were taken away. Years Six and Seven were also worried about their futures. He felt that the government kept changing its policies. This meant that when parents contacted the teaching team, they were unsure of the expected response, which made things difficult.

During lockdown, he had an important birthday, but his family was unable to go on the holiday they had planned. It also meant that their house move was put on hold, although he did believe they were lucky to have a house and garden.

Based on his scientific background, he said, 'the NHS did not crumble, money poured in, and the bureaucracy was slashed, which meant that the process of finding a vaccination could work quicker.' However, he commented, 'The new normal will be more anxiety and uncertainty.'

Memory 37

She also worked in a boarding school as a member of the support staff and so was furloughed. However, some of the children were unable to go home, but luckily, as the school's approach was holistic the house mistress setting up extracurricular activities for them.

Her husband was able to work from home and that made such a difference. They formed a 'bubble' with their

daughter and grandson, so she was able to see her
grandson every day. Other family or friends they saw
online, when they held quizzes, although she did miss
seeing them face to face. Their neighbours were
'shielding,' and missed their family terribly.

It was lucky that it was nice weather. She and her
husband redeveloped their garden and so did their
neighbours. At five o'clock each day, they stopped and
had a drink with them. This over the fence arrangement
they called their 'Beer Club.' She thought they probably
drank too much during lockdown. Seeing their
neighbours over the fence helped them all and they
became very close.

When she needed to go to the shops in Bishops Cleeve,
she walked. She thought that Tesco was very good, but
she did not think the same of Lidl. Tesco, she felt had a
system and she liked the fact that everyone had to queue.
Even so, like everywhere else, the shop seemed to
struggle with flour and toilet rolls.

When things started to go back to normal, she was able
to go back to work and felt as if now she could eat as
many biscuits as she wanted to rather than rationing
herself. Also, as soon as the Lido in Cheltenham
opened, they went as they had feared that it would not
reopen at all after lockdown. The clubs too reopened but
with less people as everyone wanted to keep socially
distancing.

During lockdown she thought the community really came together.

Memory 38

As an IT specialist at a school in Cheltenham, she helped the teachers learn Microsoft Teams so lessons could be given online.

On her last day before lockdown, her colleagues gave her some tadpoles for her children to keep them entertained during the weeks that lay ahead before they returned to school.

At home, the family each used Teams, but as they were renovating their house, they had to all work in one small room which was noisy. They invested in some earphones so they could not hear each other, but even so, they occasionally connected to the wrong device and found themselves in the wrong person's meeting.

They also met friends and family on Teams or Zoom. One friend started selling a skincare range, so she posted everyone samples and they had a 'pamper evening' online! They also had quizzes, so that helped fill the weekend evenings.

When there was a family birthday, they would all buy a cake and arrange a video call. After singing 'Happy Birthday,' they would all blow the candles out and eat the cakes together on the video call. They also had quite a few children's parties online, which included a dance party and a science party…. everyone became quite inventive!

They found different ways to socialise. She sometimes made herself a cup of tea and stood on the pavement to chat to the person across the road, pausing their conversation when cars went past. They dared not cross the road as they were in different households. It was surprising how normal this became.

They joined the trend of decorating their front window with rainbows, in support of the NHS and essential workers and the family loved walking round the village seeing these. As a family, they also cycled as in the first lockdown there were very few cars about. At 8pm every Thursday evening, they also clapped and banged for carers, the children became quite excited and could hear people round the corner doing the same.

In the early days the Government only allocated one hour a day outside for exercise so, as a family, they embraced this and discovered the beautiful local walks. But if these took longer than an hour, she worried that someone might notice. Inside the house they exercised to Joe Wicks, an online fitness coach.

The children were constantly trying to find different ways to entertain themselves and they started taking fruit and vegetables from the kitchen and turning them into pets. This became very difficult, as she was then not allowed to use them to cook with as they had names! Eventually they bought a dog as did a lot of people. She was a perfect distraction to the monotony of home schooling and lack of socialisation for the children.

Epilogue

2020 was a very strange year for the UK and Gotherington. One hundred years since the last pandemic, it was in some ways not too dissimilar.

Many people died across the country as well as some here in the village. Public Health England reported that the death rate was significantly related to health, age, gender, and ethnicity.[12] Initially, no one advising government really knew what to do for the best and just as in the last pandemic, no one knew how long it would last and, of course, just as before, there was no vaccine,at least initially.

For those that lived alone, many suffered from isolation, loneliness, and depression. Even when restrictions were relaxed, some people, whatever their age, still felt unwilling to go out. What, if anything, will be the psychological impact on them and those in education, we cannot yet know. While others believed things were not as bad as they were made out to be and that an atmosphere of fear had been created.

There was also the question of paying bills. In years gone by, there would have been no financial help from government. Yet in 2020, the government provided many businesses with grants to furlough their employees. Of course, some employees were 'let go', to

---

[12] www.gov.uk/government/publications/covid-19-review

use an Americanism, and some businesses went bankrupt or simply closed. In August 2020, the government tried to help hospitality with 'Eat out to Help Out.' However, it was suggested by some that the scheme may have led to an increase in Covid infections.[13]

Just as during the Spanish Flu pandemic, Anglican churches and other places of worship closed, but unlike 100 years ago, most people in Gotherington either had online or telephone access or both. This enabled Reverend Reakes to reach his parishioners in one form or another and to give them spiritual support.

Luckily, in the village, support was also available in the form of GOWNS, at least one voluntary responder and neighbours. These people took others to doctors or hospital appointments, offered help with IT and made available a list of local services that could be accessed via the telephone or online, as well as shopping for those isolating or vulnerable.

Online shopping became a problem in the early days. Slots at supermarkets were snapped up and became unavailable for those who really needed them. Supermarkets also had problems with the supply of certain goods, which led to some rationing for a short while. Yet, many found these items were still available from the smaller shops, that did not have the same footfall as supermarkets. This enabled smaller shops to

---

[13] The Economic Journal, Thiemo Fetzer April 2022

flourish and people to acknowledge their value to the community. Click and collect online also helped.

Some businesses thrived, and The Post Office found it was busier than ever delivering parcels to people who had ordered items online. This was true of all delivery operations.

Working and staying at home led many to enjoy the slower pace of life that lockdown brought. Those that could work from home did. Few went far, and then only when necessary. Although, for those who did have to travel it could be an anxious time if they were stopped by the police as they had the ability to fine people if they felt the journey was unnecessary.

Schools, just as a 100 years ago, closed, only this time it was not just some but all. In 2020, learning continued but went online rather than in person, although special arrangements were made for 'Key Kids.' Some clubs, too, continued online throughout lockdown and the sterling work of the NHS was acknowledged across the country.

Here in Gotherington, people were stoic and just got on with it as best they could. Others reminisced about their childhood, or that experienced by older generations, when it was safer for children to cycle around the village without the fear of fast traffic, and when families sat down to eat meals or play games together. 2020 meant that many families were able to re-enact this.

It helped that the weather during the spring and summer was exceptional and having gardens people enjoyed being in them. Many of the memories people shared were of their time in the garden. In general, people said their gardens had never looked better. They had the time to spend on them and with little else to do, the inclination to do so! In many towns and cities people did not have this luxury.

There was also VE Day, a highlight for the village in an otherwise awful year. Strings of bunting were hung outside houses and across hedges to celebrate. Tables were moved to front gardens and tea and cakes, even wine and nibbles were enjoyed by the many households who took part.

By late autumn, the weather had changed. It was now often wet and windy. Covid was on the up and government restrictions were back in place. This somewhat last-minute decision, particularly, impacted on Christmas travel and celebrations. It meant that many family members and friends, who lived further away, could not visit.

Luckily by the New Year, a vaccine had been produced. A vaccine offered some way of stopping or at least lessening the power of the virus. It had been too late for many people, and some did not believe in its efficacy. This would lead to confrontations in towns and cities in the coming year. However, for most, the vaccine was a relief, a light at end of the tunnel.

It was hoped it would not be long before some normality would be resumed. Masks could be cast aside; churches would throw open their doors and groups of people would be able to socialise again. By the end of 2020, people had realised, if they did not before, what was important to them, and this was usually family.

Some questions however, remain would things have been different if the weather had been awful throughout the year and what if a greater range of food had been scarce or rationed?

However, most importantly, unlike 100 years ago, some very clever people and the technology of the day was able to develop a vaccine which would soon be available to everyone.

Village Photographs of VE (Victory in Europe) Day

References

BBC NEWS Hayley Mortimer 30th April 2020

Celebrityinsider.org, Suzy Kerr 12th APR 2020

Evening Standard, Kit Heren 7th May 2020

IGA, 26th March 2020

Medical News Today Hannah Flynn 28th October 2021

Sky News Sophy Ridge 1 June 2020

The Today Programme, 31 March 2020

The Economic Journal, Thiemo Fetzer April 2022

www.gov.uk/government/speeches

www.gov.uk/government/publications/covid-19-review

www.gov.uk/guidance/coronavirus-covid-19-information-for-the-public

www.nhs.uk/coronavirus or www.gov.uk/coronavirus

www.ons.gov.uk

www.who.int/emergencies/diseases/novel-coronavirus-2019/advice-for-public

Plus, various local and national newspapers